SpringerBriefs in Population Studies

Population Studies of Japan

The world population is expected to expand by 39.4% to 9.6 billion in 2060 (UN World Population Prospects, revised 2010). Meanwhile, Japan is expected to see its population contract by nearly one third to 86.7 million, and its proportion of the elderly (65 years of age and over) will account for no less than 39.9% (National Institute of Population and Social Security Research in Japan, Population Projections for Japan 2012). Japan has entered the post-demographic transitional phase and will be the fastest-shrinking country in the world, followed by former Eastern bloc nations, leading other Asian countries that are experiencing drastic changes.

A declining population that is rapidly aging impacts a country's economic growth, labor market, pensions, taxation, health care, and housing. The social structure and geographical distribution in the country will drastically change, and short-term as well as long-term solutions for economic and social consequences of this trend will be required.

This series aims to draw attention to Japan's entering the post-demographic transition phase and to present cutting-edge research in Japanese population studies. It will include compact monographs under the editorial supervision of the Population Association of Japan (PAJ).

The PAJ was established in 1948 and organizes researchers with a wide range of interests in population studies of Japan. The major fields are (1) population structure and aging; (2) migration, urbanization, and distribution; (3) fertility; (4) mortality and morbidity; (5) nuptiality, family, and households; (6) labor force and unemployment; (7) population projection and population policy (including family planning); and (8) historical demography. Since 1978, the PAJ has been publishing the academic journal *Jinkogaku Kenkyu* (The Journal of Population Studies), in which most of the articles are written in Japanese.

Thus, the scope of this series spans the entire field of population issues in Japan, impacts on socioeconomic change, and implications for policy measures. It includes population aging, fertility and family formation, household structures, population health, mortality, human geography and regional population, and comparative studies with other countries.

This series will be of great interest to a wide range of researchers in other countries confronting a post-demographic transition stage, demographers, population geographers, sociologists, economists, political scientists, health researchers, and practitioners across a broad spectrum of social sciences.

More information about this subseries at http://www.springer.com/series/13101

Shigeki Matsuda
Editor

Low Fertility in Japan, South Korea, and Singapore

Population Policies and Their Effectiveness

Springer

Editor
Shigeki Matsuda
Faculty of Contemporary Sociology
Chukyo University
Toyota-shi, Aichi, Japan

ISSN 2211-3215 ISSN 2211-3223 (electronic)
SpringerBriefs in Population Studies
ISSN 2198-2724 ISSN 2198-2732 (electronic)
Population Studies of Japan
ISBN 978-981-15-2829-3 ISBN 978-981-15-2830-9 (eBook)
https://doi.org/10.1007/978-981-15-2830-9

This Springer imprint is published by the registered company Springer Nature Singapore Pte Ltd.
The registered company address is: 152 Beach Road, #21-01/04 Gateway East, Singapore 189721, Singapore

Acknowledgements

This work is a result of our study on the research association on low fertility, education, and employment in Asia (Principal Investigator: Shigeki Matsuda) which was supported by the Japan Society for the Promotion of Science, KAKENHI Grant Numbers 26285122 and 18H00936. Survey data from the Cabinet Office were used with the permission of the Children and Child-Rearing Administration, Cabinet Office. At our workshop and open seminar, valuable information and advices were given from Mr. Shigesato Takahashi (Meiji University), Dr. Toru Suzuki (National Institute of Population and Social Security Research), Ms. Akiko Matsue (International University of Health and Welfare), and Dr. Hyuncheol Kim (National Youth Policy Institute). When we visited Singapore, staff members from the National Population and Talent Division of the Prime Minister's Office provided us with much information on countermeasures against low fertility in Singapore, and Prof. Paulin Tay Straughan (Singapore Management University) suggested a new perspective of analysis to us. Nippon Research Center Ltd. conducted an accurate survey in Singapore where the survey environment differs from Japan. We also would like to thank all researchers in Japan, South Korea, and Singapore, for contributing to and stimulating this study.

Prologue

Low fertility is a demographic phenomenon which first occurred in Northern/Western Europe and was subsequently observed globally across a wide range of developed and emerging countries. Currently, fertility rates in many Northern/Western European countries are relatively stable, while those in Asian developed economies have dropped to the lowest levels worldwide. Total fertility rate of less than about 1.5 is classified as "very low fertility", and less than about 1.3 is classified as "lowest-low fertility". Japan belongs to the very low fertility category, while South Korea and Singapore belong to the lowest-low fertility classification.

In Europe, low fertility is regarded as a part of a series of demographic changes known as the second demographic transition. However, the character of fertility in Asia differs from Europe's demographic transition. Cohabitation and children born to single mothers are not widespread demographics because the marriage system is not fluctuating in Asia. For this reason, an increase in the unmarried population tends to lead to a decrease in the birth rate. In addition, the number of children couples have is decreasing. Moreover, a critical factor is that the demographic change in Europe is driven by the shift in individuals' values from material needs (such as economic security) to post-materialism (such as freedom of expression, self-realization, and autonomy). However, in Asia, similar changes in values have not yet occurred or, at least, values changing to post-materialism have not led to a decline in fertility. These demographic differences and motivating factors of the change in fertility rates in Asia and Europe depend on the differences in cultural background and their periods of modernization, as well as the unique social background of each country.

Such low fertility rates may cause a future labor shortage, weaken the social security system, and undermine social and economic stability in Asia, although the economic development in these countries has been remarkable so far. In Japan, the total population began to decline in the late 2000s due to a persistently low birth rate. In recent years, the population has decreased by about 200,000 per year, and low fertility has had a serious impact on the real economy. That low fertility brings about a decrease in the country's population and economic stagnation is not limited to Japan. Other Asian countries that experienced low fertility later than Japan will likely suffer from similar negative effects of it in the near future. Therefore, countries need to implement countermeasures against low fertility to restore their fertility rates to sustainable levels.

This book discusses the character and countermeasures against low fertility in Japan, South Korea, and Singapore, all of which are among Asian developed and emerging economies that have implemented powerful countermeasures for their persistent low fertility. Japan has been taking measures based on the two pillars of childcare facilities and work–life balance since the mid-1990s. The countermeasures in South Korea started in the mid-2000s and, like Japan, promoted support for balancing work and child-rearing and expanded childcare services. Singapore, which started the measures earlier than either country, has expanded various advanced measures such as marriage support and generous financial support for families raising children. However, none of these countries has seen a full-fledged recovery in fertility rates despite such countermeasures.

This book presents the characteristics of each country's society and the outline of countermeasures taken for low fertility and discusses why fertility in each country has not yet recovered. The following points are addressed. Was the target of the implemented countermeasures matched to the needs of the parents who were raising children? The work–life balance support and child-rearing support have been promoted together in each country. However, did they significantly increase the number of children women wanted and had? Furthermore, the reasons why the fertility rate has not improved at all are the economic obstacles and working environment for marriage and child-rearing. However, are young people starting to avoid marriage and parenting regardless of those policies?

The chapter structure of this book is as follows. Chapter 1 discusses Japan's countermeasures for low fertility implemented from the 1990s to the first half of the 2010s, including its features, problems, and required directions. Chapter 2 discusses, based on the measures to reduce the birth rate in South Korea, determinants of the gap between desired number of children and actual/expected number of children by analyzing the survey data in both South Korea and Japan. Chapter 3 analyzes the characteristics of the fertility change in Singapore by ethnicity and occupation, and Chap. 4 discusses the reasons why Singapore continues to have a low fertility rate while implementing various marriage and childcare support measures from the perspective of education and subsequent career development.

This book presents the results of collaborative research conducted by our group of interdisciplinary researchers in sociology, demography, and economics. It was supported by the Japan Society for the Promotion of Science, KAKENHI Grant numbers 26285122 and 18H00936. The quantitative analyses regarding Japan and South Korea used secondary data, while the Singapore survey was original data. To write this book, we conducted public seminars in Japan and South Korea and conferred with other researchers. We have visited Singapore and discussed with government officials working on the measures against low fertility and local researchers. The knowledge gained from this research is included in this book.

The findings of this study will provide new perspectives for effective future policymaking not only for Japan, South Korea, and Singapore but also for other Asian countries and even other regions experiencing low fertility rates. It also provides a new analysis perspective to researchers studying the declining birth rate in Asia.

Shigeki Matsuda

Contents

Chapter 1
Characteristics and Problems of the Countermeasures Against Low Fertility in Japan: Reasons that Fertility Is not Increasing

Shigeki Matsuda

Abstract Japan has had unacceptably low fertility since the mid-1970s, but the government did not officially recognize low fertility as a problem and initiate countermeasures against it until the early-1990s, when the low fertility was spurred by the "1.57 shock." For about 20 years, policy designed as a countermeasure has been based on two pillars: increasing the number of childcare facilities and supporting a desirable work-life balance. However, the total fertility rate remains low because of a mismatch between the main targets of policy: couples in which both partners are regular employees, particularly in big cities, and the actual reasons for low fertility. These reasons are: (1) increasing hesitation among young adults to get married because of deteriorating employment opportunities and (2) the heavy financial burdens on families where mothers are either homemakers or part-time workers and on families that face the dual burden of childrearing and educational costs. Therefore, in addition to the childcare and work-life balance approach, policies likely to increase fertility should focus on lightening the financial burdens of parenthood and education and on improving employment options and opportunities for single young adults.

Keywords Low fertility countermeasures · Childcare facility · Work-life balance · Education cost

1.1 Fertility Trends in Japan

Countermeasures against low fertility consist of policies designed to increase fertility by removing obstacles to childbearing. This chapter discusses the characteristics of Japanese policy, problems associated with it between the 1990s and the early 2010s, and directions needed in the future. Since the second half of the 2010s,

S. Matsuda (✉)
Chukyo University, Nagoya, Japan
e-mail: matsuda_z113@yahoo.co.jp

S. Matsuda (ed.), *Low Fertility in Japan, South Korea, and Singapore*,
Population Studies of Japan, https://doi.org/10.1007/978-981-15-2830-9_1

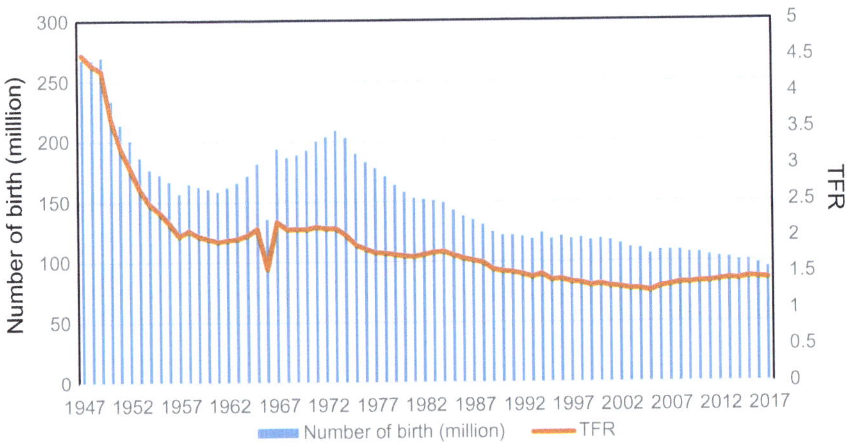

Fig. 1.1 Number of births and TFR in Japan, 1947–2017 (Ministry of Health, Labor and Welfare 2018)

the Japanese government has focused on "*Hataraki-kata kaikaku* (ways to work reforms)" and "*Kyouiku musho-ka* (no-cost education)," but, as these ongoing efforts have not yet been evaluated, they are not addressed in this chapter.

The figure illustrates the number of births and the total fertility rate (TFR) in Japan between 1947 and 2017 (Fig. 1.1). Between 1947 and 1949, an initial baby boom occurred in which the numbers of births exceeded about 2.7 million per year. In the following decade, the numbers of births dramatically decreased in response to the government's popularization of family planning, but more than two million babies were born each year between 1971 and 1974, which was a secondary baby boom. Since then, the number of births has gradually decreased, and in 2018, only about 918,000 babies were born, which was about one-third the size of the first baby boom.

Between the mid-1950s and the mid-1970s, after an initial plunge after the first baby boom, the TFR fell to a point near population replacement level. After the mid-1970s, the TFR dropped further and is now the lowest TFR that Japan has experienced in many decades, below replacement level.

It is important to note that the TFR was 1.58 in 1966, which was the "*Hinoe-uma*" (Fire-Horse) year, which comes once every 60 years in the Japanese zodiac. Many couples avoided childbirth in that year because of the superstitious belief that women born in that year would not be marriageable because they would have temperamental natures. The belief was widespread in Japan, and the TFR in 1966 was much lower than in the preceding and following years. The extent of the influence of this superstition on the TFR was surprising at the time because Japan had recently held the Tokyo Olympic Games in 1964 and was becoming a global economic power supported by science and technology.

Low fertility in Japan has thus been a continuous phenomenon for more than 40 years. However, the Japanese government was slow to consider the declining TFR as a problem. Then, in 1990, the "1.57 shock" occurred, in which the TFR of the previous year fell below that of "*Hinoe-uma*" for the first time. The government was shocked and responded by officially recognizing low fertility as a problem and instituting countermeasures against it. However, despite these efforts, the TFR continued to fall and, in 2005, it reached 1.25, the lowest rate in recorded history. Thereafter, fertility began to gradually increase, but, 12 years later, in 2018, it still was just 1.42, which was lower than before the countermeasures were implemented. Why was fertility persistently low and sluggish, even long after the countermeasures had been implemented? The answer to that question might be found by examining Japan's countermeasures, which is the subject of this chapter.

The chapter is structured as follows: Sect. 1.2 presents the history of the countermeasures against low fertility in Japan and describes their characteristics, Sect. 1.3 explains the effects of the countermeasures and their limitations, and in Sect. 1.4, a suggested future direction for countermeasures is set out.

1.2 History of Low Fertility Countermeasures

1.2.1 Early Countermeasures

The government's first plan to counter low fertility was the Angel Plan in 1994, which recognized the following causes of low fertility: (1) increased opportunity costs of parenthood as women entered the workforce, (2) the difficulty of balancing parenthood with paid employment, (3) the psychological and physical burdens of childcare, (4) housing conditions and birth trends, and (5) costs of education. The plan set out measures to support parenthood, such as: promoting support for balancing childrearing and work, childrearing support at home, improvements to housing and living environments to accommodate childrearing, realization of pressure-free education and sound development, promotion of childcare cost reduction, and reduced costs of childrearing. At the time, the reasons understood for the low fertility and the focuses of the countermeasures were multifaceted. However, to implement the Angel Plan, the "Emergency childcare measures 5-year project" of 1994 was created to increase the number of childcare facilities, particularly for preschool children, extend childcare facilities, provide regional-level support facilities, and so on. Basically, a major aspect of the Angel Plan was the "childcare facility," and that focus characterized the direction of all subsequent measures.

In 1999, the Angel Plan and the five-year project were reviewed, which led to the Basic Policy for the Promotion of Countermeasures to the Declining Birthrate (Basic Policy) and the New Angel Plan. While a focus on childcare facilities remained at the core of countermeasures, new target areas included employment, maternal and child health, consultation, and education. During that period, a policy was undertaken to increase the number of childcare facilities and eliminate waiting lists, which continues to be a governmental strategy for improving childcare facilities.

1.2.2 The Pillars of Childcare Facilities and Work-Life Balance

Policy Related to Childcare Facilities

After the *Shoshika Shakai Kihon Hou* (Basic Act for Measures to Cope with a Society with a Declining Birthrate) and the *Jisedai Ikusei Shien Taisaku Suishin Hou* (Advancement of Measures to Support Raising the Next Generation of Children Act) were passed in 2003, various low fertility countermeasures were promoted. These were based on two pillars: childcare facilities and work-life balance. The government's white papers on the low fertility at the time summarized the countermeasures as being based on both pillars.

The first pillar was the expansion of childcare facilities to follow government standards and offer subsidies.

The Basic Policy and the 2004 *Shoshika Shakai Taisaku Taikou* (Outline of Measures to Cope with Society with Declining Birthrate) set forth the guidelines of the countermeasures based on the Basic Policy. Childcare facilities were given a central focus in the Basic Policy and the Outline. The Outline stated that Japan would work to eliminate waiting lists at childcare facilities by systematically increasing their capacities, mainly in metropolitan cities with many waiting children. In addition, it supported women's employment as a countermeasure, clearly stating in the Basic Policy that Japan would enrich women's employment by adding benefits, such as childcare leave, to support their desires to enjoy rich family lives while maintaining fulfilling work lives. It should be noted that the emphasis was on supporting women's employment rather than providing employment opportunities to young adults. The financial situation of young adults was not considered in the Basic Policy, while it was mentioned in the Outline. Situations in which young adults were finding it difficult to achieve socioeconomic and social independence and unemployment or were "freeters" (individuals who lack full-time employment or are unemployed, excluding homemakers and students) were mentioned, but those concerns were not believed to be linked to the low fertility.

Three other plans soon followed: *Kodomo Kosodate Ouen Plan* (Childrearing Support Plan) in 2004, *Kodomo Kosodate* (Childrearing Vision) in 2010, and Plan to Reduce Childcare Facility Waiting Lists in 2013. Along with the *Kodomo Kosodate kanren 3 hou* (Three Related Childrearing Laws) in 2012, a new system was launched in 2015 to increase the number of childcare facilities and childcare operations at kindergartens. Key measures concerned expanded childcare services.

These successful childcare measures increased the numbers of childcare facilities. The capacity of these facilities was about 1.9 million and the number of children using them was about 1.92 million in 2003; in April of 2017, there were 27.5 thousand facilities serving 2.55 million children. Thus, although the number of children born each year continues to decrease, the childcare facility uses rate by preschool children increased from 27 to 42% between 2003 and 2017 because of the increased availability of childcare facilities. In particular, the government increased the capacity of childcare facilities for children aged 0–2, for whom there had previously been insufficient capacity compared with ages 3–5.

During the past 10 years, the numbers of children on waiting lists was about 26,000 each year, but it was easier than before for mothers to use the facilities. This is because these facilities had expanded beyond the metropolitan areas and the Osaka region into rural areas. In addition, previously, it had been difficult for mothers with non-regular jobs to use the facilities for children younger than three years, but that situation changed when the regulations surrounding childcare facilities changed. It was not counted as the number of waiting children in the past if a child of the parent extending a childcare leave for not deposit a child at a childcare facility and was looking at the child at home, which was the reasons why the number of waiting children has not decreased apparently for the time.

Facilitating Mother's Work-Life Balance

The other pillar of the countermeasures was a desirable work-life balance. The government launched a directive to include reviewing ways to work with men and supporting childrearing in the area, in the measures that focused on childcare facilities. This was the *Shoshika Taisaku* Plus One (Countermeasures against low fertility Plus One Plan) of 2002. Based on that *Jisedai Ikusei Shien Taisaku Suisin Hou* (Law for Measures to Support the Development of the Next Generation) law was enacted in 2003. It formulated action plans for businesses and local governments to support workers, particularly women who were working and raising children. Under the 2003 Law, businesses that developed action plans and achieved their goals were certified as Childrearing Support Companies, a status that qualified them for certain tax incentives, such as extra amortization of buildings. The 2003 Law was 10-year timed legislation, which was extended in 2014 for an additional 10 years.

Tackling the work-life balance problem was considered indispensable for solving the conflicts between employment and motherhood that women faced. *Kodomo to Kazoku wo Ouensuru Nihon Juten Senryaku* (The Strategy to Assist Children and Families) and the Top Conference for Promoting Work-Life Balance were created in 2007, the latter comprising representatives of political labor and management to formulate the Work-Life Balance Charter. The activities developed by this conference are ongoing.

The above-stated policies had various influences on women's work-life balance. First, the childcare leave system was expanded. *Ikuji Kyugyou-tou ni kansuru houritu* (The Childcare Leave Law) came into force in 1992, and it was revised several times after that. Currently, employers have to grant their employees childcare leave until their child is one year old (under certain conditions up to two years old if the parent is not using childcare facilities). During childcare leave, employees can receive 67% of their monthly incomes from employment insurance (50% after six months from the start of childcare leave). There also is the Papa & Mama Childcare Leave Plus System that allows for childcare leave of up to 14 months when both parents use the childcare leave. Furthermore, the Childcare Leave Law obliges employers to provide benefits, such as short workdays (six hours per day) for workers with children younger than three years old. Under the *Jisedai Ikusei Suishin Taisaku Hou* (Law for Measures to Support the Development of the Next Generation) of 2003, companies are encouraged to implement support for employees who have a child, such as no overtime days, shortened and flexible working hours, and childcare facility in the workplace.

According to Matsuda (2013), from an international perspective, countries whose public burden ratio (i.e., the amount of taxes and social insurance fees) is high, such as the Scandinavian countries, tend to enhance their social welfare and labor policies because a high national burden ratio is necessary to implement those policies. On the other hand, in the USA and other countries where the public burden ratio is low, public childcare facilities and childcare leave, which are meant to be individuals' responsibility, have not been developed. Considering that Japan's public burden ratio is much lower than in many European countries, the countermeasures described above, which the Japanese government has recently implemented, have been generous policies. No other developed Asian countries have established similarly generous systems.

1.2.3 Characteristics of Conventional Countermeasures and New Directions

A range of perspectives and measures were included, but Japan's low fertility countermeasures have mainly focused on the two pillars of childcare and work-life balance. Who were the main beneficiaries of these policies?

Childcare facilities in Japan are meant mainly to allow people to raise their children while they work. Couples in which both partners have regular employment benefited most from the provision of childcare facilities for children aged 0–2. On the other hand, those who have become effective targets of the work-life balance policy are also couples in which both partners enjoy regular employment. Owing to concrete work-life balance countermeasures implemented by companies for regular employees, such as no overtime workday, shortened and flexible working hours, and childcare facilities in the workplace; women of non-regular employees with children, who have traditionally had shorter working hours, do not tend to make use of these newly implemented measures. Taken together it can be concluded from the above that the main target of Japan's low fertility countermeasures was the two-income married couple who were regular employees with a preschooler.

In addition, the previous countermeasures were mostly applied in large cities since the shortage of childcare facilities was serious there and large enterprises that promoted and led the way toward providing work-life balance benefits tended to be located there.

In recent years, the two pillars dominating policies in this regard have gradually changed. *The Shoshika Kiki Toppa Task Force* (Task Force against low fertility) in 2014 under the minister responsible for low fertility suggested that marriage, pregnancy, and childbearing support should be a third pillar of the countermeasures in addition to childcare facilities and work-life balance. In response, support for marriage, which previously had been the financial responsibility of local government, was incorporated into the menu of the countermeasures. The Outline of 2004 was revised in 2015 to add policy to support marriage and multi-generational households and to strength the countermeasure by local circumstances, etc. In 2014, the *Machi Hito Shigoto Sousei Hou* (law of regional revitalization) was intended to strengthen municipal economies and communities as a new approach to the countermeasures. To prevent the emigration of young adults from rural area and shrinking rural populations, the policy encouraged local governments to determine ideal total population sizes, implement ways to arrest population declines, and facilitate industrial relocations to rural areas.

1.3 Evaluating the Countermeasures

1.3.1 Outcomes and Limitations of the Measures

More than 25 years have passed after the government began implementing low fertility countermeasures. What are the results to date?

In 2004, the Ministry of Internal Affairs and Communications (MIAC) evaluated the countermeasures (Ministry of Internal Affairs and Communications 2004) that focused on mothers' burdens when balancing work and childcare and found that they generally had been eased, but that women's sense was that the burden of motherhood was not lighter, particularly among homemakers. The reason for this lack of improvement was a belief that the financial burdens of childrearing and education had increased. The MIAC further concluded that the countermeasures had not been successful in their efforts to increase fertility.

More than fifteen years have passed since the MIAC's evaluation, but those conclusions still apply to the subsequent measures. Building more childcare facilities and supporting ways to achieve a desirable work-life balance certainly have occurred. The number of childcare facilities has significantly increased as described above; a childcare leave system and shortened workdays for regular employees raising children have also been developed. Women with preschool children who are regular employees, particularly those who work during pregnancy and after childbirth, have been the primary recipients of these benefits.

However, other countermeasures have progressed very little. There has not been much support for mothers who are homemakers or part-time workers and support has been weak for young single adults who need employment opportunities. Child allowances, similar to those in some major European countries to mitigate the financial burdens of childrearing, have not been implemented in Japan.

The most important concern is that the countermeasures have failed to boost fertility, which was their original purpose. Japan has been working on these countermeasures ever since the government decided that low fertility was a problem when it fell below the "*Hinoe-uma*" year's TFR of 1.58. It was expected that the TFR would have increased after the countermeasures were implemented in 1994, but it continued to decline to 1.26 in 2005. It has gradually been increasing since then, but it was still below replacement level at 1.42 in 2018. If the current TFR level does not change, Japan's provincial populations will soon begin shrinking. The fear is that eventually the Japanese population will disappear entirely, possibility that has recently been seriously evoked.

When discussing TFR level, it is worth noting that for a long time, no official TFR target existed for the countermeasures. This is because the government feared criticism based on the pre-World War II political campaign of "*Ume-yo Huyase-yo* (Beget and Multiply)." However, Japanese demographics are very different from the period before the War when childbearing was encouraged. By not setting a target TFR when it first implemented the countermeasures, Japan's government allowed the purposes of the policy appear obscure, and this reduced the effectiveness of policy. In 2016, the government finally set a target TFR of 1.8 by 2025 to be achieved by fulfilling the people's needs regarding marriage and childbirth.

1.3.2 Mismatch Between the Main Policy Targets and the Actual Situation in Japan

The reason that fertility did not increase in response to the countermeasures can be understood by considering the characteristics of the two main pillars of the low fertility countermeasures: improved childcare and work-life balance.

Let us review the main points of what we discussed in the previous section. Historically, the majority of children on the childcare facilities' waiting lists have been aged 0–2 years (about 90% of them in 2017) and their mothers tended to be regular employees. Accordingly, the facilities' capacities for this particular age group were increased. Further, childcare leave and short workday policies have exclusively benefitted mothers with regular employment. In other words, the countermeasures have focused on mothers who are regular employees and work during pregnancy and after childbirth. As regular employees, they use childcare leave, childcare facilities, and short workdays. These mothers are in couples where both partners hold regular jobs. The question then becomes: how many couples have these characteristics in Japan?

Before responding, it is important to consider the influence of marriage on the TFR. The proportion of unmarried Japanese men and women aged 25–34 years has been increasing since the 1970s (Fig. 1.2). The trend has slowed, but not stopped, since the 1990s when the countermeasures took effect. In Japan, marriage is closely tied to the TFR because non-marital childbearing is extremely rare, and about 90% of the TFR decline since the mid-1970s can be explained by the decline in marriage rates (Iwasawa 2015). The main reason for the decline since the 1990s has been deteriorating employment opportunities for young adults, which was a different problem from the childcare facilities and childcare leave.

Let us go back to the previous question about the proportion of mothers who are in regular jobs. Previous research revealed that many Japanese women stop working when they get married or become mothers. The proportion of women who continue to work after marriage or after their first child, regardless of their access to childcare leave, was consistently about one in four from the late 1980s until the second half of the 2000s (Fig. 1.3). In other words, majority of Japanese women leave their jobs and become homemakers when they have a child (at least for a period of time). The continuous employment rate of females who gave birth in the first half of the 2010s has risen to 38% (National Institute of Population and Social Security Research 2017). However, these figures reflect that more than half of these women still stop working when they marry or become mothers. Another survey by the Japan Society of Family Sociology showed similar results; the National Family Research of Japan (NFRJ) revealed that, in 2008, women with children younger than six years old comprised 14% of all regular employees, 24% of all non-regular employees (including self-employed and where the majority were "part-time workers"), and 61% of all homemakers (Matsuda 2016). Clearly, most Japanese mothers of young children were not regular employees in their childrearing period.

It is noteworthy that the definition of part-time work, which is one of a type among non-regular employment, is somewhat different in Japan than in Western countries. Part-time work is chosen not to interfere their homemaking and parenthood responsibilities by mothers prioritizing family life. Therefore, employee's typical work hours are several hours per day, and their wages are relatively low. And, these employment contracts tend to be less than one year.

Regarding changes to the Japanese family (including changes to the mothers' way of working), family sociologists in Japan have used the above NFRJ data to test the following two hypotheses. (1) The structural fluctuation hypothesis: The number of typical of Japanese families, comprised of a married couple with children in which there is a gendered division of labor, decreased. Instead, households comprised of married couples where husband and wife are employed outside the home and share household and childcare responsibilities increased. (2) The structural stability hypothesis: Overall, the typical Japanese family has not markedly changed and strongly gendered divisions of labor remain typical. The NFRJ data supports the structural stability hypothesis (Inaba 2011).

These results indicate a mismatch between the main target of the countermeasures and the facts about Japanese young adults and Japanese families. It is obvious that the TFR would not increase simply by supporting a portion of people who are

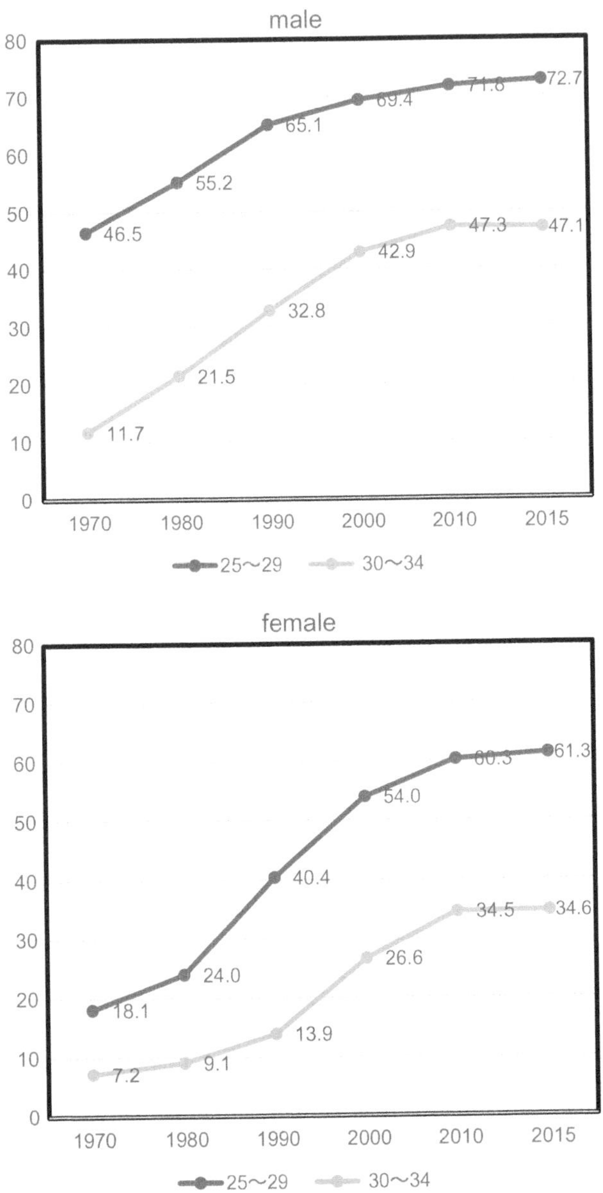

Fig. 1.2 Unmarried rate by gender and age (Naikakuhu 2018)

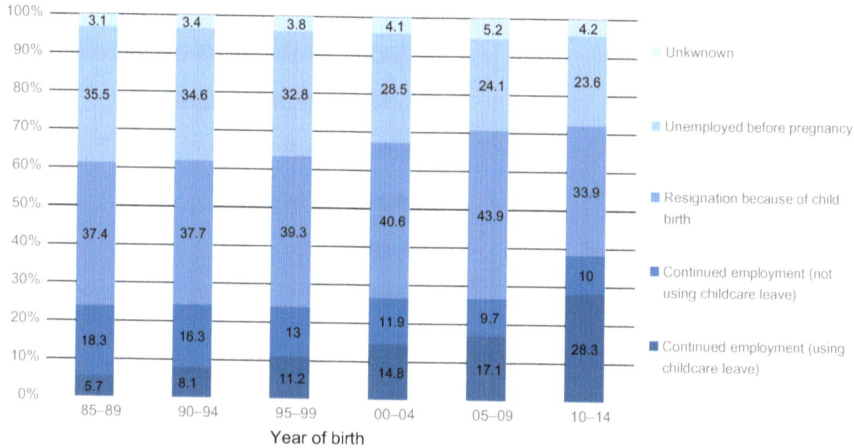

Fig. 1.3 Women's employment during pregnancy and after first birth. *Source* National Institute of Population and Social Security Research (2017)

two-income, married couples with regular jobs, and preschool children on whom the countermeasures focused. Some of the architects of the countermeasures might have assumed that the TFR would increase if the number of childcare facilities was increased and a desirable work-life balance facilitated, expecting that the countermeasures would encourage full-time homemakers, women who were part-time employees, and young adults in non-regular employment to marry, have children, and continue to work fulltime. However, the results imply that most people did not respond as anticipated.

1.3.3 Reasons that Couples Do not Have the Ideal Number of Children

The ideal number of children per couple in Japan is 2.32, but couples' planned number of children is only 2.01 (National Institute of Population and Social Security Research 2017). Decrease in the number of children a couple have is one reason for Japan's low fertility. Figure 1.4 lists the reasons that Japanese want few children. The most common reason was "It costs too much to raise and educate children" (56.3%), which was much more common than the second most common reason. So important was this reason that it would appear that financial assistance for childcare and children's education is vital in promoting childbearing. Furthermore, it was especially important for women who are homemakers or part-time workers, who form large proportions of all couples during the active parenting years. The second most common reason was "I do not want to give birth at an old age," followed by "I was unable to get pregnant even though I wanted to."

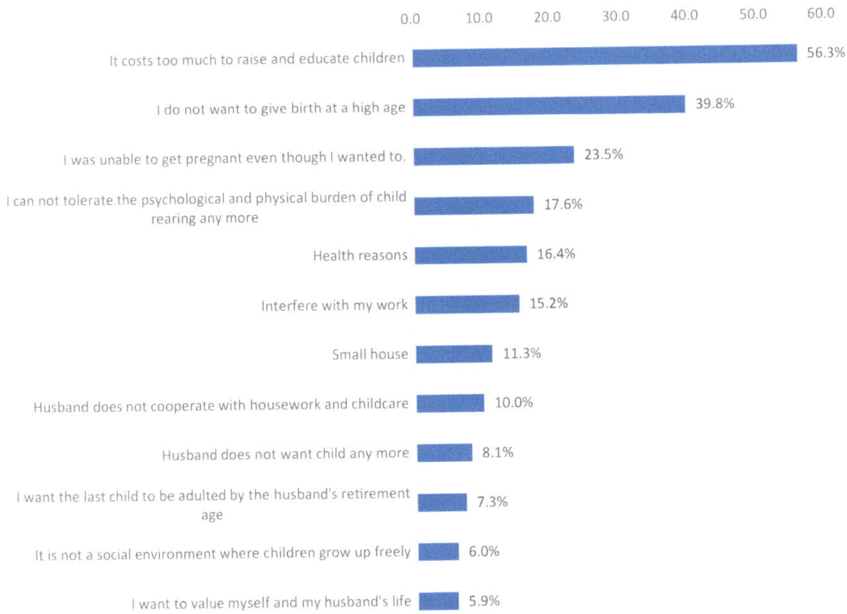

Fig. 1.4 Reasons that couples do not have the ideal number of children (National Institute of Population and Social Security Research 2017)

These reasons are related to the increase in marriage age, which is brought about by the fact that young people cannot get married due to poor employment prospects. In sum, these results suggest that policies to increase the TFR in Japan should focus on easing the financial burdens on childrearing and education and supporting marriage in young adults.

1.4 Changed Paradigm and Expanded Policy Targets for the Future

The historical and current theoretical framework, which is a theoretical paradigm, recognizes that the number of women that want to work during pregnancy and childrearing has increased along with women's social advancements (Matsuda 2013). In that context, the shortage of childcare facilities and insufficient support of a desirable work-life balance offered by employers, such as childcare leave, has invited low fertility. The paradigm has provided a theoretical basis on which the countermeasures comprising childcare and work-life balance as the main pillars have been built for a long time. However, as explained above, the countermeasures have addressed only some of the aspects of Japan's low fertility.

Now, Japan must make a paradigm shift to be consistent with the facts explaining low fertility over the past 20 years and take effective countermeasures to restore the fertility level. In 2013, the author (Matsuda 2013: 225) pointed out the following concerns.

> The increase in the number of people who cannot get married because of deteriorating employment opportunities for young adults and the fact that childbearing and childrearing are becoming difficult for typical Japanese families which occupy a large part of family during childcare, are the main causes of low fertility. Insufficient compatibility between work and childcare by societal factors such as a shortage of childcare facilities and insufficient childcare leave, was mainly concerned by couples with regular employment living in big cities.

In this chapter's introduction, the low fertility countermeasures were defined as policies to increase the TFR by removing obstacles to childbearing. To promote those countermeasures, Japan needs to expand its policy targets to include the following: (1) unmarried young adults, (particularly those with few employment opportunities), (2) married couples in which the wife is either a full-time homemaker or a part-time worker, and (3) married couples in which both partners are regular workers (particular urban residents). Specifically, Japan should first focus on enhancing the employment opportunities of single young adults, such as job creation and vocational training. In addition, married couples where the woman is a homemaker or part-time worker, particularly those with many children, need enhanced financial support in the form of child allowances, reduced (subsidized) educational costs from early childhood education through to higher education, childcare support centers, low-cost childcare options. Support is also needed for mothers returning to work after a child-related leave. In addition to childcare support, corrective measures such as eliminating mandatory long work hours and facilitating a work-life balance could help the third target.

References

Inaba, A. (2011). Trends and future direction of the Japanese family: Analyses of NFRJ (National Family Research of Japan) 98, 03, and 08 data. *Japanese Journal of Family Sociology, 23*(1), 43–52.

Iwasawa, M. (2015). Shoshika wo motarashita Mikonka oyobi Huuhu no Henka (Decline of marriage rates and change to couples causing low fertility). In S. Takahashi & H. Ohbuchi (Eds.), *Jinkou Gensho to Shoshika Taisaku (Depopulation and countermeasures against low fertility)* (pp. 49–72). Tokyo: Hara Shobo.

Matsuda, S. (2013). *Shoshika ron: Naze mada kekkon shussan shiyasui kunini naranainoka* (The theory of the declining birth rate: Why isn't Japan a society in which it is easy to marry and give birth?) Bunkyo-ku: Keiso shobo.

Matsuda, S. (2016). *Chichi-oya no ikuji sanka no henyou* (Changes in father's childcare participation). In I. Akihide, T. Yasuda, R. Tabuchi, & S. Tanaka (Eds.), *Nihon no Kazoku 1999–2009: Zenkoku Kazoku Tyousa [NFRJ] ni yoru Keiryo Shakaigaku (Japanese family 1999–2009: Quantitative Sociology using National Family Survey [NFRJ])* (pp. 147–162). Tokyo: Tokyo University Press.

Ministry of Health, Labor and Welfare (MHLW). (2018). *Vital Statistics*.
Ministry of Internal Affairs and Communications (MIAC). (2004). *Shoshika Taisaku ni kansuru Seisaku Hyokasho (Policy evaluation report on measures against low fertility)*.
Naikakuhu (Cabinet Office). (2018). *Heisei 30 nendo shousika-shakai Hakusho (White paper of countermeasures against low fertility in Heisei 30)*. Tokyo
National Institute of Population and Social Security Research (NIPSSR). (2017). *Marriage and childbirth in Japan today: The Fifteenth Japanese National Fertility Survey, 2015*.

Chapter 2
Determinants of the Gap Between Desired and Actual/Expected Number of Children in Japan and South Korea

Ji-Hey Bae

Abstract The purpose of this study is to investigate the determinants of the gap between attitudes toward family size and actual/expected family size in Japan and South Korea. This study found that there is a gap between the desired and actual/expected number of children in both Japan and South Korea. Furthermore, the following common points and differences between the two countries were observed as factors that influence the discrepancy. In both Japan and South Korea, the employee benefits and family-related factors had no effect. It was observed that employment status was a point of difference between the two countries. In Japan, the gap was smaller for women employed regular workers than for unemployed women. By contrast, in South Korea, the woman's employment status had no significant effect. This result suggests that the targets of countermeasures for low fertility will be different in each country. Finally, the effect of attitude-related factors was different in Japan and South Korea. However, there is a possibility of simultaneity bias in the association between having the desired number of children and attitudinal variables; therefore, it is necessary to be mindful of the causal relationships between variables. Future research might focus on the methodological problems, including validating the possibility of simultaneity bias.

Keywords Family size · Gap between ideal and reality · Work-related factors · Attitude-related factors

2.1 Introduction

Since the so-called "1.57 shock" in 1990, Japan's total fertility rate continued to fall, and in 2005, recorded its lowest value ever at 1.26. During subsequent years, it gradually increased, and the total fertility rate announced by the Ministry of Health, Labor, and Welfare was 1.44 as of 2016. However, the fact remains

---

J.-H. Bae (✉)
J. F. Oberlin University, Tokyo, Japan
e-mail: jiheybae@obirin.ac.jp

S. Matsuda (ed.), *Low Fertility in Japan, South Korea, and Singapore*,
Population Studies of Japan, https://doi.org/10.1007/978-981-15-2830-9_2

unchanged that Japan's rate is low compared to the fertility rates of other advanced OECD countries. The situation in South Korea is even more serious. South Korea's total fertility rate was 1.31 in 2001 and continued to fall to 1.08 in 2005. A series of small increases and decreases followed, and as of 2016, the total fertility rate had settled at 1.17.

Even though the low fertility continue, for many couples in Japan and South Korea, the desired number of children is now greater than the actual number. For example, Fukuda (2014) used "Longitudinal Surveys of Adults in the Twenty-first Century," published by the Ministry of Health, Labor, and Welfare, to compare the average values for desired and actual number of children in each age group, and clearly demonstrated that a large gap existed between these categories for all groups. In Japan, as observed from the average values for desired and actual number of children, achieving the desired number of children is not a simple matter. In South Korea as well, as evidenced in the childbearing population, the average desired (or ideal) number of children is 2.0–2.3, which is the level required for population replacement, also known as replacement fertility level (Lee and Park 2015). Also, 65.7% of Koreans, who had completed their families after one child, responded that the ideal number of children was two or more (Cha 2005). Furthermore, the fact that 27.1% of married Korean people, who had reached the end of their reproductive life reported giving up on having their desired number of children (Bae and Kim 2012), demonstrates that a discrepancy exists between attitudes about family size and actual fertility, as in Japan.

Many of the recent studies on low fertility comment that eliminating this discrepancy, namely creating an environment where individuals could have their desired number of children, is a policy issue faced by low fertility societies (Fukuda 2014; Lee and Park 2015; Hyundai Research Institute 2010; Nishimura 2012). Therefore, the present study considers the problem of low birthrates in Japan and South Korea by focusing on the discrepancy between the attitudes toward family size and the reality, using statistical methods to analyze the factors causing the discrepancy.

2.2 Policy Response in South Korea

This section prefaces the literature review with a brief overview of South Korean population policies that are related to the country's low fertility rate. As the Japanese policy is explained in detail in Chap. 1, it will not be referenced here.

Several previous studies hold that South Korean population policy relating to the country's low fertility rate may be broadly divided into three categories (Kim 2019; Woo 2018): (1) an initial phase of anti-natalist policy, followed by (2) a phase of quality improvement, and finally (3) a pro-natalist phrase (Table 2.1).

When the first of these phases, population control policy, began in the 1960s, South Korea had recently passed through a period of upheaval that included independence from 36 years of Japanese colonial rule as well as the Korean War.

Table 2.1 Classification of population policy in South Korea

Classification	Period	Details
Population control policies	1962–1995	Preparation of family planning program (1962–1966)
		Institutional provision of family planning program (1967–1971)
		Diversification of population control policies (1971–1981)
		Strengthening of population control policies (1982–1988)
		Completion of population control policies (1989–1995)
Population quality improvement policies	1996–2004	Rectification of imbalanced sex ratio at birth and prevention of induced abortions
		Improvement of family health and well-being and response to sex-related problems among young people
		Increasing female employment and labor efficiency
		Intervention in existing family planning programs and policies supporting antinatalism
Low birth rate and aging population policies	2005–present	First Basic Plan for Low Fertility and Aging Society (2006–2010)
		Second Basic Plan for Low Fertility and Aging Society (2011–2015) Third Basic Plan for Low Fertility and Aging Society (2016–present)

Sources Woo (2018) and Kim (2019)

Growth of the country's struggling economy was presented as the issue of utmost importance at that moment. The South Korean government at the time considered a policy for the regulation of population growth, as well as advanced population control measures that aimed to solve overpopulation, vital to the viability of its economic development plan. Specific policies included the widespread distribution of contraceptives, financial support for sterilization, and educational initiatives to raise public awareness (Matsue 2012). While these population control policies subsequently underwent various degrees of revision under successive governments, they continued into the mid-1990s.

The repressive aspect of the family planning programs of this period, that were state-led and lacking in consideration for individual human rights (reproductive rights), is undeniable. Nevertheless, the state's population control policies did correspond to the desires of individuals to control birthrates in the pursuit of intragenerational and intergenerational social mobility, and the South Korean population decreased at a rapid rate (Woo 2018).

However, the speed of this decrease far surpassed initial expectations, and concerns were raised over its abnormal rate at the beginning of the 1990s. This triggered a thorough investigation into the results of the country's population control policies to date and the various implications that could stem from future changes in the size and composition of the population. Ultimately, the South Korean government overhauled its policy in 1996, moving from previous population control policies to a new population policy that aimed to improve the population's composition and well-being. This reflected specialist organizations' opinions that population control policies did not favor future national economic development. As outlined in Table 2.1, this new policy, in contrast to the previous family planning program and anti-natalist policies, focused on issues such as the achievement of a balanced sex ratio at birth, the prevention of induced abortions, responding to sex-related problems among young people, and the improvement of family health and well-being.

However, it is uncertain whether these measures ought to be strictly interpreted as relating to population quality. There are indications that the South Korean population policy of this period was less focused on population quality and more focused on undergoing a "transitional period" during which it was impossible to establish the direction (Woo 2018: 44). In a similar vein, some hold that the new population policy of this period demonstrated neither explicit awareness of the issues presented by the low fertility rate, nor the policy efforts needed to support the birthrate necessary for sustainable social and economic development (a goal of the new policy), making it no more than the end of existing population control policy (Matsue 2012: 38).

However, when low fertility rates emerged in the 2000s as a contributor to the rapid aging of the population, South Korean population policy became actively pro-natalist, in a complete reversal of its previous stance. For example, in 2005, the Basic Law on Low Fertility and Aging Society was drawn up and implemented, forming the legal basis for policies related to low fertility and the aging population. In 2006, the Basic Plan for Low Fertility and Aging Society was created as a comprehensive measure targeting the declining birthrate and the aging population. This plan was taken on by 15 government ministries, including the Ministry of Health and Welfare and the Division of Labor (now called the Ministry of Employment and Labor) (Do 2018).

South Korea's Basic Plans for Low Fertility and Aging Society covered periods of five years (Table 2.2). The First Basic Plan, which formed the initial phase of establishing low fertility policy, prioritized the creation of an environment conducive to childbirth and child-rearing, through initiatives that supported areas classed as vulnerable in terms of childbirth (Kim 2019). However, support for childcare services, and policies for the reduction of the financial burden chiefly targeted those in the lower-income bracket (earning 70% or less than the average urban worker's income, or 100% or less for families with two working parents). Results were limited by the inability to cover dual income households requiring childbirth and childcare support and the fact that nongovernmental organizations, including businesses, could not be involved. As a result, the Second Basic Plan aimed to adopt a comprehensive approach that supported a work–family balance extending to dual income households and the middle class, and which was provided by society as a whole—including business and citizen participation—rather than by the government alone (Do 2018; Matsue 2012).

Table 2.2 Summary of the basic plans for low fertility and aging society

Category	First (2006–2010)	Second (2011–2015)	Third (2016–2020)
Vision	Construction of a favorable environment for birth and child rearing	Building the basis for a gradual recovery in birth rates	Achieving a sustainable, developed society where all generations can be happy together
Aims	1. Removal of factors presenting obstacles to birth and child rearing	1. Normalization of a work-family balance.	1. A happy society with children
	2. Expansion of social support networks for the healthy growth of children and young people	2. Alleviating the burden of marriage, childbirth, and child rearing	2. A productive and dynamic aging society
		3. Creation of an environment supporting healthy growth of children and young people	
Driving Factors	• The burden of child rearing and school fees	• Declining population and large-scale shift to an aging population	• Policy responses taking into consideration the drastic decline in childbirth and speed of aging population that remained insufficient (need for increasing basic awareness of the issues around changing population makeup as well as long-term countermeasures)
	• The difficulty of balancing work and family	• Continual deferment of marriage and childbirth due to social and economic factors	• Necessity of pooling capacity from all sectors of society for a crisis response to the "population precipice"
	• Childcare support facilities that provide adequate environments for child rearing		

Source Do (2018)

However, in spite of these efforts, birthrates continued to fall. Against this backdrop, the Third Basic Plan, in operation since 2016, determined that the First and Second Basic Plans were inadequate for the task of restoring birthrates and tackling low fertility problem in the long term. This approach understands the causes of low fertility in terms of social structure, such as employment, education, and housing and emphasizes the necessity of improving these factors.

As explored above, South Korean policy regarding the country's low fertility rate can be described as having moved from an initial antinatalism to pronatalism, in response to the social change created by low fertility and weakened family functioning. In addition, support that initially targeted vulnerable groups has recently widened in scope to cover all families (Do 2018). Nevertheless, South Korea's birth rate is yet to show any signs of recovery. Therefore, the challenge for future policy is to attempt to solve the issue through a paradigm shift from state-led fertility policy targeting the birthrate and number of births, to a human-centered policy that improves the quality of life and respects the right of an individual to choose his or her own way of life (Presidential Committee on Aging Society and Population Policy).

2.3 Previous Studies

2.3.1 Definition of Key Terms

First, this study will clarify the definitions of the key terms, "desired number of children" and "expected number of children." Desired number of children is defined as the fertility consistent with an individual's wishes, as long as there are no factors impeding fertility (Bae and Kim 2012). By contrast, expected number of children is the number of children a couple actually intends to have. The difference between these terms is that the desired number of children does not depend so much on individual circumstances and various restrictions on its achievement, such as the wishes of one's spouse. Those types of restrictions are strongly reflected in the expected number of children (Fukuda 2014; Iacovou and Tavares 2011).

2.3.2 Factors that Explain the Gap Between Desired and Actual/Expected Number of Children

The factors explaining the gap between desired and actual/expected number of children can be categorized into workplace-related, family-related, and attitude-related factors.

First, Van Peer (2002) analyzed Fertility and Family Survey (FFS) data, and clearly demonstrated that in countries, such as Spain, Italy, and Poland, part-time working,[1] women with unstable employment exhibited the largest gap between

---

[1]According to Van Peer (2002), part-time work is defined as working up to 34 h per week. However, it is necessary to note that the definition of part-time work differs by country. In Japan, for example, part-time work is not always distinguished from full-time work (regular employment) by the number of working hours alone. According to Osawa (2004), in addition to working hours,

desired and actual number of children. The results of previous studies found that the greater the status in terms of stable employment, such as regular full-time workers and employers, the higher the desired number of children, but also that form of employment is not only relevant in terms of increasing the desired number of children (Kong 2006), it is an important factor for actually having the desired number of children. Meanwhile, in Austria and Sweden, the greatest mismatch between the desired and actual number of children was found in women who had stable full-time employment, and the probability that unemployed women would achieve their desired number of children was lower than for women who worked part-time. Van Peer (2002) interprets these results as caused by good access to high-quality part-time jobs in Sweden, which may enable women to achieve a balance between work and home life.

According to Nishimura (2012), who used data from the international comparative study conducted in 2010 by the Cabinet Office of Japan, which surveyed families in the USA, France, Sweden, South Korea, and Japan, husband's working hours have a positive impact on the achievement rate of desired fertility in the USA and Japan. This result was interpreted to indicate that when a man worked longer hours, his income also increased. However, in light of the increasing trend of two-income households in both Japan and South Korea (Cabinet Office of Japan 2017; Statistics Korea 2016), and research findings indicating the negative effect of a woman's long working hours on birthrates (Shigeno 2006), it is necessary to study the effect of wives' (not just husbands') working hours on both the desired number of children and fertility.

The possibility exists that, in addition to form of employment and working hours, various workplace policies supporting childbirth and childcare will have an effect on the desired and actual/expected number of children. For example, Lee and Moon (2017) studied married working women who did not yet have children, and found an association between the existence of maternity and childcare-related policies, such as those providing prenatal/postnatal leave, childcare leave, and childbirth incentives, and the level of women's awareness about these policies, with the intention of having a first child. Shigeno (2006), who analyzed the effect of childcare leave policies on women's fertility, obtained results in Japan indicating a higher rate of first births among women who worked at companies with childcare leave policies than among unemployed women, and claimed that when the childcare leave policies were effective, they could positively contribute to both women's jobs and maternity/child-rearing. Although these studies did not directly analyze the gap between the desired and the actual/expected number of children, they suggested the possibility that workplace assistance, which is related to childbearing and child care, had the effect of closing this gap, because it might influence both a woman's intention to have children and her childbearing behavior.

---

full-time work and part-time work are distinguished by career management differences. Full-time employees have various obligations to the company (e.g., overtime work, relocation, etc.). On the other hand, there are no such obligations for part-time workers. As a result, there is a big difference in the degree of employment security between part-time work and full-time work.

Next, family-related factors, such as whether a couple resides in the same household with their parents or how child-rearing responsibilities are divided between spouses, also affect the gap between the attitudes toward family size and the actual situation. According to Lee and Park (2015), who defined the "fertility gap" as the difference between the desired and the actual number of children, and analyzed the factors affecting this difference, the fertility gap became smaller when unemployed people, other than the mother and father, lived in the same household and cared for the children. Although the study did not analyze the fertility gap itself, Park (2008) reported that a woman's intention to have a second child becomes stronger in relation to the amount of time her husband spends on household chores. This result corresponds with McDonald's proposition (2000), which stated that very low fertility in advanced countries is caused by an inconsistency between high levels of gender inequity in individual-oriented social institutions and sustained gender inequity in family-oriented social institutions. Based on this argument, it is certainly possible that the division of household labor between spouses has an effect on the gap between desired and actual/expected number of children.

So far, we have reviewed the previous research concerning workplace-related and family-related factors that affect the difference between desired and actual/expected number of children. However, it is not only attitude factors that affect the birth of the desired number of children, but also subjective factors as well. For example, Bae and Kim (2012) analyzed the effect that traditional South Korean family values, such as son preference, gender role attitudes, and familism, have on the birth of the desired number of children. Their results indicated that when he/she held traditional values, his/her desired number of children was higher, but conversely, his/her actual number of births was lower. These results were interpreted to indicate that traditional society views childbirth as a more important role for parents than child-rearing. It is thought that the more children the better, but raising children is a heavy burden in modern society, and if there is no appropriate child-rearing environment, couples give up on having their desired number of children.

Furthermore, Lee and Park (2015) clearly demonstrated that individuals' views toward government childbirth incentive policies consistently exerted a positive effect on elimination of the fertility gap. Specifically, if people considered pro-birth policies "very successful," the probability of eliminating the fertility gap was 48.5% higher than if people considered them to be "very unsuccessful." In Japan, Matsuura (2008) reported that the difference between the ideal and actual number of children changed depending on where the responsibility for child-rearing was placed. People who think that national and local public organizations should be responsible for childcare tend to have a wider gap between ideal and actual number of children, and this tendency is particularly pronounced in females.

Based on this prior research, this chapter analyzes the workplace, family, and attitude factors that determine the gap between attitudes toward family size and actual/expected births in Japan and South Korea, both societies with critically low fertility.

2.4 Methods

2.4.1 Data

The data used in this study was obtained from the "The Comparative Research Study on Provisions for Declining Birthrate in Regions of Asia (South Korea, Japan, and Singapore)," which the Japanese Cabinet Office conducted in 2008. Women under the age of 50 with at least one child (352 in Japan and 322 in South Korea) were chosen for the analysis.

2.4.2 Variables

2.4.2.1 Independent Variables

For work-related factors, this study used employment status (unemployed, regular employee, non-regular employee, and self-employed), working hours per week (including commuting time), and employee benefits used in child-rearing ("maternity leave from work," "childcare leave," "paternity leave," "shorter working hours," "nursing leave for children," and "childcare centers established by companies for employees"). Under the employee benefits category, each of the employee benefits used received a score of 1, while each that was not used received a score of 0.

Under family-related factors, the categories were living with one's parents and division of housework. If one lived with their own or their spouse's parents, a score of 1 was assigned, while if one lived separately, a score of 0 was assigned. For division of housework, the categories "done exclusively by the wife," and "wife mainly does it but the husband also helps out" were rated as "wife mainly does it" and assigned a score of 1. The categories "wife and husband do about the same amount," "husband mainly does it, but the wife also helps out," and "done exclusively by the husband" were rated as "husband and wife share equally/ husband mainly does it," and assigned a score of 0.

Finally, for attitude-related factors, this study used responses to questions about so-called "myth of the first three years[2]" and primary responsibility for fertility rate decline problem. First, regarding the "myth of the first three years," if the response to the opinion that "the mother should take care of the child at home without using daycare services, etc. until the child is about three years old" was "strongly

[2]The myth of the first three years states that "When the child is young, the mother should stay close to her child up to three years old and concentrate on childcare" (Ohinata 2015: 72). It is said that the myth of the first three years was established in postwar Japanese society against a backdrop of scientific research (hospitalism studies, Bowlby's Maternal Deprivation Theory, etc.) and changes in socioeconomic conditions, including industrial structure transformation, population structure conversion, urbanization, and the growth of nuclear families (Takayama 2002).

disagree" or "somewhat disagree," a score of 1 was assigned and "strongly agree" or "somewhat agree," a score of 0 was assigned. Concerning primary responsibility for fertility decline, the question was asked, "Which party should be responsible for dealing with the continuous decline in the fertility rate, or decline in birthrate problem?" If the response was "each and every citizen," a score of 1 was assigned, whereas if the response was "the national government, local governments, regional societies/civic organizations, corporations and labor unions," a score of 0 was assigned.

2.4.2.2 Dependent Variables

This study used three questions[3] to create the following categories: (1) women who had given birth to the desired number of children; (2) women who want to have more children up to the desired number of children; (3) women who will not/cannot have more children than the desired number of children. The gap between desired and actual/expected number of children was then analyzed as the dependent variable.

Among these three categories, "a match exists between the desired and actual/expected number of children" in two of the categories. They are (1) "women who had given birth to the desired number of children" (= a match between the desired and actual number of children) and (2) "women who want to have more children up to the desired number of children" (= a match between the desired and expected number of children). By contrast, it can be said that (3) "women who will not/cannot have more children than the desired number of children" represent cases where "the desired and actual/expected number of children do not match." In this study, the dependent variables were created by assigning 1 to the former, "a match exists between the desired and actual/expected number of children," and 0 to the latter, "the desired and actual/expected number of children do not match," and a binary logistic regression analysis was performed.

2.4.2.3 Control Variables

As control variables, this study used factors, such as age, age at first marriage, age of youngest child, years of education, household income, and residence, all factors which had been identified in previous studies as affecting the gap between desired

[3]The survey measured desired number of children using the responses to the question, "How many children would you like to have, in total? If you already have children, please include them in your answer." Also, the number of actual children is requested in the question, "How many children (including adopted children) do you have in total?" To women who replied that their desired number of children was greater than their actual number, the next question was asked, "Which of the following statements best describes your desire to have more children?" to inquire about their desire for additional children.

and actual number of children. Descriptive statistics of the variables used for analysis are shown in Table 2.3.

There are no significant differences between Japan and Korea in terms of basic attributes, including: age, first marriage age, educational age, and household income. Working hours are slightly longer in Korea, but the use of employee benefits is remarkably low. Women are mainly responsible for housework in both countries. The major differences between the countries have to do with: employment status, living with parents, place of residence, and attitude factors. Compared to Korea, Japan has a higher non-regular employment ratio, and it has a higher rate of parents living with their adult children. It is also interesting to note that over 90% of respondents affirm the claims of the myth of the first three years. Belief that the responsibility for low fertility does not lie with individuals is also high.

2.5 Results

2.5.1 *The Gap Between Actual and Desired/Expected Number of Children*

There was a difference between Japan and South Korea for the current and desired number of children (Fig. 2.1). Looking at the current number of children in both the Japanese and the South Korean groups, the majority had "2 children," followed by "1 child" and then "3 or more children," in descending order. However, the percentage of women with "2 children" in the South Korean group was higher than in the Japanese group. On the other hand, even though there was a slight difference in the desired number of children in the Japanese group, "3 or more children" was ranked higher than "2 children" and had the highest percentage overall. By contrast, in the South Korean group, the percentage that answered "2 children" was almost double that for "3 or more children."

Looking at the mean values for current and desired number of children, the desired number of children in Japan was 2.5 and in South Korea it was 2.3. In both countries, the desired number of children exceeded replacement level.[4] By contrast, the current number of children was 2.0 in Japan and 1.9 in South Korea. In both countries, the desired number of children was higher than the current number of children. When Japan and South Korea were compared, both the current and desired number of children were higher in Japan, and for desired number of children in particular, the difference was statistically significant.

[4]As of 2015, the Japanese replacement level was 2.07, and while we do not have the most recent Korean data, it is 2.08 according to Engelman (2006), who used 2005 UN data.

Table 2.3 Variables used in analysis

	Japan		South Korea	
	M	SD	M	SD
Age	37.0	6.5	39.8	5.6
Age at 1st marriage	25.1	3.3	25.9	2.9
Age of youngest child	7.0	5.8	11.1	6
Years of education	14.1	2.2	13.6	2
Household income (per year)[a]	487.6	238.5	409.2	169.9
Working hours per week	17.4	18.8	22.9	26
Employee benefits[b]	0.4	0.9	0.3	0.7
(%)				
Employment status	Regular employee (12.5)	Non-regular employee (25.3)	Regular employee (21.4)	Non-regular employee (9.0)
	Self-employment (11.9)	Non employment (50.2)	Self-employment (16.1)	Non employment (53.5)
Live with parent	Yes (29.5)	No (70 5)	Yes (9.0)	No (91.0)
Division of house work	Mainly wife (93.9)	Others (6.1)	Mainly wife (90.4)	Others (9.6)
Myth of the first 3 years	Agree (66.6)	Disagree (33.4)	Agree (90.3)	Disagree (9.7)
Primary responsibility for fertility decline	Each and every citizens (38.4)		Each and every citizens (24.4)	
	Others (61.6)		Others (75.6)	
Residence	Tokyo 23 wards, ordinance-designated city (23.9)		Seoul special city (46.6)	Others (53.4)
	More than 100,000 of the city (39.2)			
	100,000 below city (26.7)	Counties (10.2)		

[a]Japan = 10,000 Yen, South Korea = 100,000 Won
[b]Among "maternity leave from work," "childcare leave," "paternity leave," "shorter working hours," "nursing leave for children," and "childcare centers established by companies for employees,"
1 = each of the employee benefits used, 0 = while each that was not used
Note The data used are both the International Opinion Survey on a Low Birthrate Society

Next, we examine the gap between the desired and actual/expected number of children in Japan and South Korea (Fig. 2.2). In Japan, 29.9% of the subjects responded, "I will not/cannot have more children to the desired number of children," and 70.1% responded, "I had given birth to the desired number/wish to have

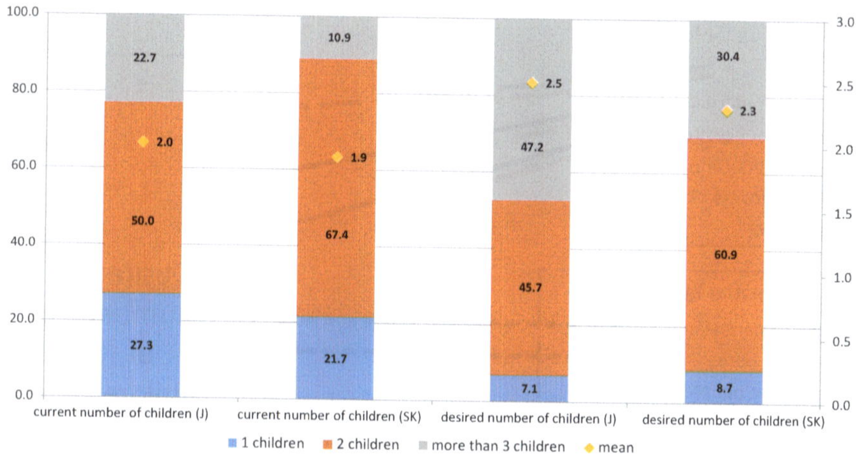

Fig. 2.1 Current and desired number of children. *Note* The data used are both the International Opinion Survey on a Low Birthrate Society

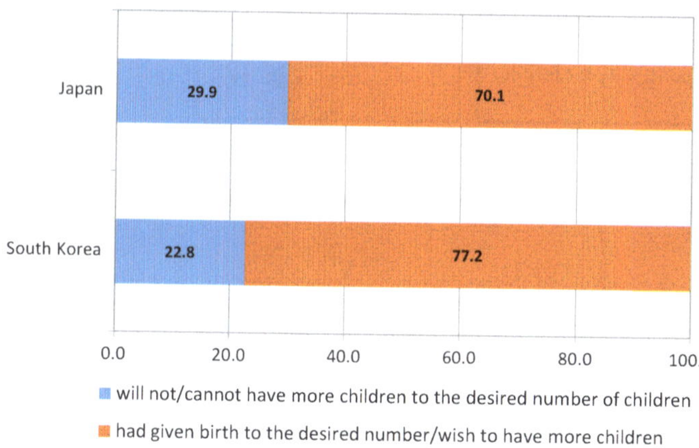

Fig. 2.2 Gap between desired and actual/expected children. *Note* The data used are both the International Opinion Survey on a Low Birthrate Society

more children." On the other hand, in South Korea, the former was 22.8% and the latter 77.2%. The gap between the desired and actual/expected number of children was greater in Japan than in South Korea. It is believed that these data reflect the result that the desired number of children was significantly higher in Japan than in South Korea.

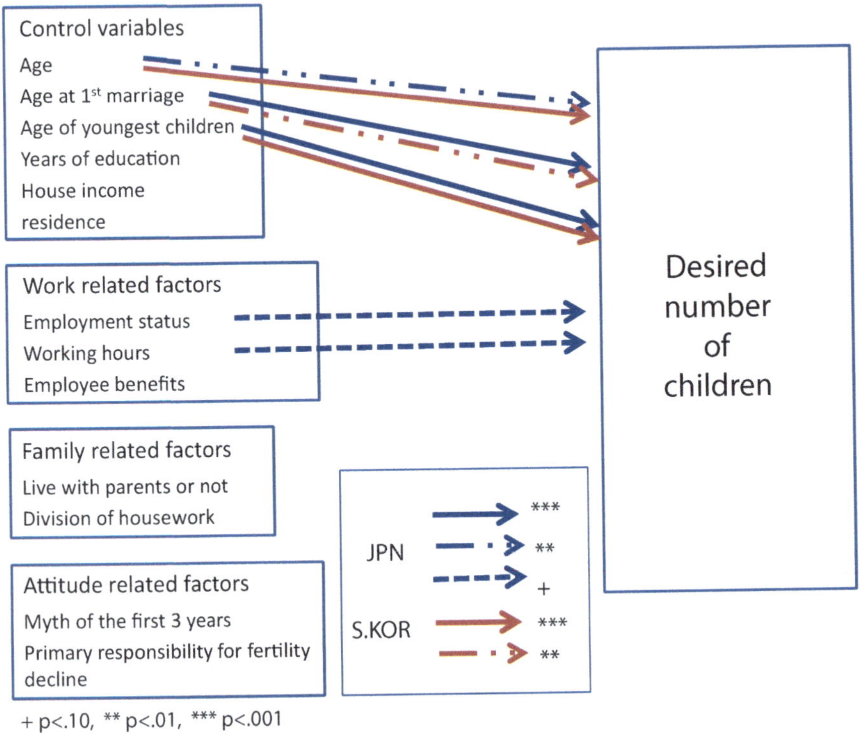

Fig. 2.3 Results of multiple regression analysis with desired number of children as the dependent variable

2.5.2 *Factors that Cause the Gap Between Attitude and Reality*

As a preliminary step in analyzing the factors that determine the difference between desired and actual/expected number of children, this study investigated the factors that influence the desired and actual number of children. We performed multiple regression analysis[5] with the desired and actual number of children as dependent variables, for Japan and South Korea, respectively (Figs. 2.3 and 2.4, see Appendix for details).

The higher the age, the lower the age at first marriage, and the lower the age of the youngest child, the greater the desired number of children in Japan and South Korea. Both employment status and working hours had a significant effect in Japan.

[5]Before implementing the multiple regression analysis, in order to determine multicollinearity, as a result of studying the correlation coefficient among independent variables, we did not see a high enough correlation coefficient (0.90 or greater) for multicollinearity, so I decided to apply a regression model to all of the independent variables.

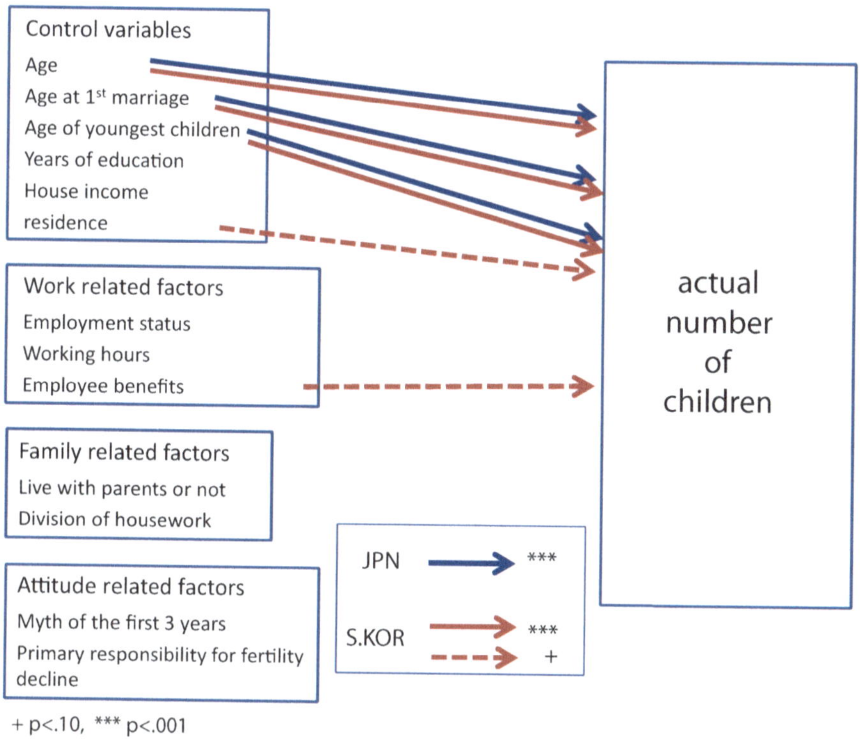

Fig. 2.4 Results of multiple regression analysis with actual number of children as dependent variable

Regular employment and long working hours exerted a negative effect on the desired number of children.

In both Japan and South Korea, age, age at first marriage and age of youngest child influence actual number of children (Fig. 2.4) and represent the same results as the desired number of children. However, in Japan, the effect of employment status and working hours observed for the desired number of children was no longer observed in the analysis of actual number of children. By contrast, in South Korea, the effect of employee benefits was observed. Based on these results, it could be said that the more employee benefits used, the greater the actual number of children in South Korea.

From the above information, the desired and actual number of children, compared to the control variables, such as age, age at first marriage, and age of youngest child, and either work-related, family-related or attitude-related factors, had absolutely no effect. While considering these points, this study performed binary logistic regression analysis using the gap between desired and actual/expected number of children as dependent variables (Fig. 2.5, see Appendix for details).

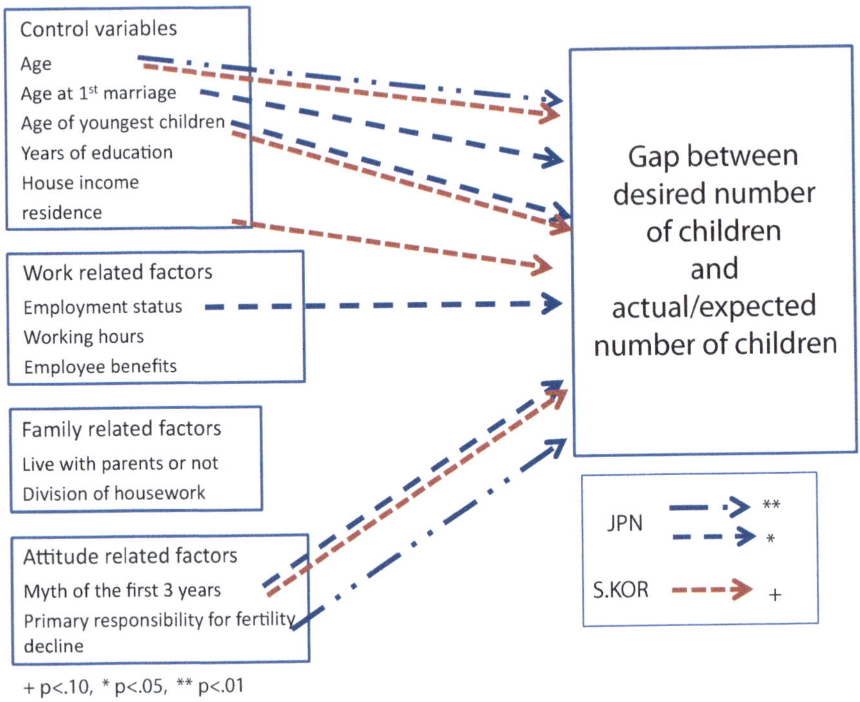

Fig. 2.5 Binary logistic regression analysis using gap between desired and actual/expected number of children as dependent variables

Considering the results for Japan, and similar to the two analysis results mentioned above, the factors age, age at first marriage, and age of the youngest child still exerted a significant effect, but attitude-related factors, such as views about the "myth of the first three years" and responsibility for fertility decline also had a significant effect. For the factors the higher the age, the lower the age at first marriage, and the lower the age of the youngest child, then the smaller the gap between the desired and expected number of children. The regular employment, for which a significant effect was observed on the desired number of children, had only a single significant effect among the work-related factors. When a woman was a regular employee, a smaller gap occurred between the desired and expected number of children, compared to an unemployed woman. We did not observe an effect from employee benefits used at work, nor did we find variables in family-related factors that had any significant effect. In our analysis of the desired and actual number of children, among the attitude-related factors, for which absolutely no significant effect was observed, this study found some interesting results for two factors that did have a significant effect. Specifically, the more a woman disagreed with the "myth of the first three years" and the more she thought individuals were responsible for the low fertility, the smaller the gap between her desired and the actual/expected number.[6]

Meanwhile, there were few variables that exerted statistically significant effects in South Korea as compared with Japan. The effect of age at first marriage, which had affected the desired and actual number of children, was also lost. If the woman did not live in Seoul or a Metropolitan city, and the higher the age, the younger the age of her youngest child, then the smaller the gap between her attitudes toward family size and her actual situation. Within work-related factors and family-related factors, there were no variables exerting statistically significant effects. Of the attitude-related factors, attitudes about the "myth of the first three years" had a significant effect. Overall results showed that if the woman did not live in Seoul or a Metropolitan city, the woman was older, her youngest child was young, and if she agreed with the "myth of the first three years," then the gap did not occur.[7]

2.6 Discussion

2.6.1 The Discrepancy Between the Ideal Family Size and the Reality in Japan and South Korea

The point of departure for this chapter was an awareness of the problems in having the desired number of children, which represents a critical policy issue in a low fertility society. The results found a gap between the desired and the actual/expected number of children in Japan and South Korea. Furthermore, the gap is larger in Japan than in South Korea. This result reflects that, even though there was a difference in distribution between Japan and South Korea concerning the current number of children, a large difference was not observed, but the desired number of children was higher in Japan than in South Korea. In any case, in both countries, the desired number of children exceeds the replacement level. This study found that the requirement for future countermeasures for low fertility is not about increasing the desired number of children, but rather about the need to create a social environment where the desired number of children can be born.

---

[6]There are no significant differences between: the desired versus the actual number of children, depending on whether a Japanese woman agrees with the myth of the first three years, whether she thinks that individuals are responsible for low fertility. However, if she disagreed with the myth of the first three years, and she thought that individuals were responsible for low fertility, she tended to answer that she wanted to have more children, up to her desired number of children.

[7]There are no significant differences between: the desired versus the actual number of children; whether a woman agrees with the myth of the first three years; where, in Korea, she lives; and her youngest child's age. However, if she disagreed with the myth of the first three years, did not live in Seoul, and her youngest child was young, she tended to answer that she wanted to have more children, up to her desired number of children.

Also, as a result of analyzing the factors that determine the desired and actual number of children in Japan and South Korea, we find that, in both countries, the desired and actual number of children greatly depend on demographic factors, such as the woman's age, age at first marriage, and age of the youngest child. The effect of work-related factors was not that great, and both family-related and attitude-related factors had almost no effect.

2.6.2 What Is Needed to Eliminate the Discrepancy

Next, the results of our analysis of the factors that affect the gap between the desired and actual/expected number of children, principally concern work-related, family-related, and attitude-related factors. The present study observed the following similarities and differences between Japan and South Korea.

The first common point between countries was that the employee benefits women used in child-rearing did not have an effect on shrinking the gap between desired and actual/expected number of children. In South Korea, the employee benefits had an effect on the actual number of children. At the very least, as seen from these study results, even if women make use of various employee benefits that support child-rearing, those do not cause an increase in the number of children women wish to have in either country, nor do they cause women to actually increase their families to the desired size. These findings contradict the assertions of previous studies (Kong 2008; Fukuda 2014; Yamaguchi 2009) that say to solve the problem of low fertility, various services are required that positively support a balance of work and family life to enable women to have the desired number of children. In other words, our findings suggest that if we are to approach the problem of low fertility in Japan and South Korea from the standpoint of "giving birth to the desired number of children," women's work-family life balance is not the best approach. In this study, the analysis focused primarily on work-related, family-related, and attitude-related factors, but it is anticipated that future research will investigate other more diverse factors that are obstacles to achieving the desired number of children.[8]

However, it is necessary to pay attention to the fact that, in both countries, the utilization rate of almost all employee benefits was low. Therefore, before debating the effects of employee benefits to support maternity and child-rearing, it will be necessary to first investigate which employee benefits coincide with women's needs, and to think more deeply about what kind of environment will easily enable women to use these employee benefits.

[8]A representative factor is the problem of educational expenses. In fact, some studies in Korea report that the fertility inhibition effect of private education expenses is extremely high (Lee and Park 2015).

Another common point is that family-related factors did not exert a significant effect in either country. Neither living with parents nor participation by husbands in housework and child-rearing, resources that lightened the women's loads, exerted a significant effect on the birth of the desired number of children. It is possible that, depending on the health status of the respondents' parents, rather than providing assistance with housework and childcare, parents could require care themselves and so increase the women's household workload. In fact, in South Korea, even though it was not statistically significant, living with parents had a negative effect on the birth of the desired number of children.

Employment status was also found to be a point of difference between Japan and South Korea. In Japan, the more women worked at regular employment, the lower the desired number of children; however, the gap between desired and actual/expected number was smaller for regular employment than for unemployment. An overall trend was observed whereby, regardless of employment status, women who worked in some fashion, whether regular employment or self-employed, had a smaller gap between desired and actual/expected number of children. It can be inferred that for Japanese women, the merit of obtaining work (regular employment in particular) is that it demonstrates the ability to possibly increase the family size to the desired number of children. By contrast, in South Korea, the woman's employment status had no statistically significant effect on the gap between the desired and actual/expected number of children. Also, it is interesting to note that all of the codes for the variables relating to employment status are the opposite of those obtained in Japan. In other words, for South Korean women, work itself hinders the increase in family size to the desired number of children. These results are in agreement with the comment that in South Korea, the opportunity cost for women who have children is too high, and that they have no choice but to delay marriage and motherhood in order to continue working in a stable situation. The present study was unable to investigate the specifics of this opportunity cost, but when South Korean society considers countermeasures for low fertility, it will be necessary to obtain an accurate picture of these opportunity costs and to actively pursue methods to reduce them. Also, the fact that a difference between Japan and South Korea can be seen in the effect of employment status suggests that the targets of the countermeasures will be different in each country. Unemployed women in Japan and employed women in South Korea should probably be the priority targets for the countermeasures.

Another difference between the two countries was the pronounced effect of attitude-related factors in Japan. Results were obtained in South Korea indicating that the more women agreed with the "myth of the first three years," the smaller the gap between attitudes toward the desired and actual/expected number of children. Also, the effect of attitudes concerning who was responsible for handling low fertility was not statistically significant. In Japan, if a woman disagreed with the "myth of the first three years," the more she thought each and every citizen was responsible for handling low fertility, and the smaller the gap between desired and actual/expected family size. In other words, these results indicate that present Japanese society is not conducive to women having a desired number of children if they hold conservative views of child-rearing and want society (national and local governments) to deal with the low birthrate problem.

2.6.3 *Future Issues*

However, concerning the association between having the desired number of children and attitudinal variables, it is necessary to be mindful of the causal relationships between variables. According to Lee and Park (2015), who analyzed the effect of views about the South Korean government's childbirth incentive policies concerning the fertility gap, the possibility that the desired number of children was determined according to views on policies coexisted with the possibility that opinions critical of policies were formed because the fertility gap was large. In light of these comments, it is very likely that the results of this study will represent the opposite of the causal relationships between variables. Specifically, it might not be that people with innovative views on child-rearing and a belief that individuals are responsible for handling the low fertility actually had their desired number of children.[9]

Finally, as Fukuda (2014) pointed out, responses to questions about desired number of children have a tendency to be sensitive to the question format. According to his analysis, in a 10-year period, 70% of women changed their answer concerning desired number of children. In Europe and the USA, long-term studies using panel data are already underway. There are few in Japan and South Korea, but longitudinal data have been constructed. Considering the overseas trends in related research, it is time to accumulate analyses using these data in Japan and South Korea as well.

2.7 Appendix

See Appendix Tables 2.4, 2.5, and 2.6.

※Japan = 10,000 Yen, South Korea = 100,000 Won
※※JPN: 1 = tokyo 23wards, ordinance-designated city
2 = more than 100,000 of the city
3 = 100,000 below city
4 = counties

[9]Rather, it might be that people that had/or could have had their desired number of children later embraced innovative views on child-rearing and came to believe that individuals were responsible for handling the low birthrate. In order to validate these possibilities, subsequent research will be necessary to control simultaneity bias using structural equation modeling (Lee and Park 2015).

Table 2.4 Multiple regression analysis with desired number of children as the dependent variable

		Japan	Korea
		β	β
Control variables	Age	0.393**	0.465***
	Age at first marriage	−0.363***	−0.204**
	Age of youngest child	−0.643***	−0.489***
	Years of education	0.007	−0.068
	House incomes (per year)※	0.013	0.053
	Residence※※	0.086	−0.026
Work-related factors	Employment status (ref = non employment)		
	Regular employee dummy	−0.192+	−0.070
	Non-regular employee dummy	−0.037	0.013
	Self-employment dummy	−0.117	0.093
	Working hours per week	0.211+	0.048
	Employee benefits※※※	0.044	0.043
Family-rerated factors	Live with parents or not (live with parents = 1)	0.025	0.045
	Division of housework (mainly wife = 1)	0.022	0.013
Attitude factors	Myth of the first three years dummy (disagree = 1)	−0.068	0.069
	Primary responsibility for fertility decline dummy (each and every citizen = 1)	−0.030	0.067
	N	249	315
	R^2	0.157	0.104
	adj.R^2	0.103	0.059
	F	2.903***	2.311**

$+p < .10$, $**p < .01$, $***p < .001$

Table 2.5 Multiple regression analysis with actual number of children as dependent variable

		Japan	Korea
		β	β
Control variables	Age	1.423***	0.820***
	Age at first marriage	−0.766***	−0.327***
	Age of youngest child	−1.252***	−0.750***
	Years of education	0.074	−0.080
	House incomes (per year)※	−0.046	0.036
	Residence※※	0.050	−0.091+
Work-related factors	Employment status (ref = non employment)		
	Regular employee dummy	−0.026	−0.082
	Non-regular employee dummy	0.025	−0.042
	Self-employment dummy	0.018	−0.066
	Working hours per week	0.089	0.127
	Employee benefits※※※	−0.083	0.097+

(continued)

Table 2.5 (continued)

		Japan	Korea
		β	β
Family-rerated factors	Live with parents or not (live with parents = 1)	0.032	−0.002
	Division of housework (mainly wife = 1)	0.022	0.059
Attitude factors	Myth of the first three years dummy (disagree = 1)	−0.038	−0.007
	Primary responsibility for fertility decline dummy (each and every citizen = 1)	0.027	0.002
	N	249	315
	R^2	0.417	0.213
	adj.R^2	0.380	0.173
	F	11.122***	5.400***

+p < .10, ***p < .001

Table 2.6 Binary logistic regression analysis using gap between desired and actual/expected number of children as dependent variables

		Japan	South Korea
		Exp (B)	Exp (B)
Control variables	Age	1.190**	1.106+
	Age at first marriage	0.844*	0.945
	Age of youngest child	0.854*	0.909+
	Years of education	1.111	0.955
	House incomes	1.000	1.000
	Residence※	1.016	0.597+
Work-related factors	Employment status (ref = non employment)		
	Full-time dummy	7.415*	0.824
	Part-time dummy	1.506	0.793
	Self-employment dummy	3.568	0.415
	Working time	0.989	1.006
	Services used in raising children※※	0.757	0.955
Family-rerated factors	Live with parents or not (live with parents = 1)	1.377	0.877
	Division of housework (mainly wife = 1)	0.393	0.946
Attitude factors	Myth of the First Three Years dummy (disagree = 1)	2.247*	0.429+
	Primary responsibility for fertility rate decline dummy (each and every citizen = 1)	3.320**	1.089
	−2LL	248.219	295.601
	Cox and Snell R^2	0.154	0.042
	Nagelkerke R^2	0.217	0.065
	x^2	39.009**	12.505
	df	15	15
	n	352	322

+p < .10, *p < .05, **p < .01

S. Korea: 1 = Seoul special city
2 = others

※※※Among "maternity leave from work," "childcare leave," "paternity leave," "shorter working hours," "nursing leave for children," and "childcare centers established by companies for employees,"
1 = each of the employee benefits used, 0 = while each that was not used

References

Bae, G. I., & Kim, K. S. (2012). A study on the influence of family values and birth policy on the wanted fertility rate. *Korean Journal of Social Welfare Studies, 43*(3), 239–266.

Cabinet Office of Japan. (2017). *White Paper on Gender Equality 2017.*

Cha, K. W. (2005). The differences in household economic structure between low-fertility and birth-planned households. *Journal of Korean Home Management Association, 23*(2), 137–148.

Do, N. H. (2018). Dongasia (Han-Jung-Il)ui Jeocyulsan Jeongchaek Byonhwawa Jaengjeom (The change and issues of east asian countries' low fertility policy). *Korea Institute of Child Care and Institute, 59,* 38–45.

Engelman, R., & E. Leahy. (2006). How many children does it take to replace their parents?: Variation in replacement fertility as an indicator of child survival and gender status. In *Prepared for Population Association of American 2006 Annual Meeting, Session 102: New Ways of Looking at Fertility Measurement Challenges.*

Fukuda, S. (2014). Desired fertility in Japan: Evolutional patterns and outcomes over the life Course. *IPSS Working Paper Series (J)* No. 11.

Hyundai Kyoungje Yeonkuwon. (2010). *Himangjanyosuwa chulsanzanyosu kanui gyokcha haesoui haebob–Jeochulsan woninkwa taecheke daehan seolmuncyosarul jyunsimuro (Reducing the Gap Between Desired Number of Children and Actual Number of Children–Focusing the Survey about Causes and Countermeasures of Low Fertility).* HyundaiKyoungjeYeonkuwon VIP REPORT 10–24.

Iacovou, M., & Tavares, L. P. (2011). Yearing, learning, and conceding: reasons men and women change their childbearing intentions. *Population and Development Review, 37*(1), 89–123.

Kim, S. J. (2019). A critical study on the population policy of korea in the low fertility and aging society. *The Journal of the Korean Urban Geographical Society, 22*(2), 143–158.

Kong, S. Y. (2006). The influence of demographic and socioeconomic characteristics on fertility of married women after the 1997 economic crisis. *Health and Social Science, 19,* 119–149.

Kong, S. H. (2008). Il-kazok yangrib hyusilkwa chulsanseontaek (The reality of work-family balance and the choice of childbirth). *Gender Studies, 13,* 65–86.

Lee, S. J., & Moon, S. H. (2017). The analysis of factors that influence the first childbirth intentions among married working women in South Korea-focusing on working conditions and workplace pro-natal programs. *Korean Journal of Family Social Work, 55,* 129–155.

Lee, J. Y., & Park, J. W. (2015). An analysis of 'fertility gap' in Korea: Focusing on the difference between real and desired children numbers. *Korean Policy Studies Review, 24*(4), 1–32.

Matsue, A. (2012). Low fertility and policy interventions in South Korea. *Journal of Population Problems, 68*(3), 32–49.

Matsuura, T. (2008). Naniga risoukodomokazuto genjitsukodomokazuno sawo umidasunoka (What cause the difference between the ideal number of children and the actual number of children). *Japanese Journal of Research on Household Economics, 78*(1), 52–60.

McDonald, P. (2000). Gender equity, social institutions and the future of fertility. *Journal of Population Research, 17*(1), 1–16.

Ministry of Health, Labour and Welfare in Japan. (2017). *Vital Statistics in Japan.*

Morita, Y. (2006). Kosodateni tomonau disincentiveno kanwasaku (Mitigation Measures for Disincentives Accompanying Child Rearing). In Y. Higuchi (Ed.), *Syoshikato nihonno keizaisyakai (Low Fertility and Economic Society in Japan)* (pp. 49–80). Tokyo: Nippon Hyoron Sha.

Nishimura, T. (2012). *What are the factors of the gap between desired and actual fertility?—A comparative study offour developed countries*. Discussion Paper No. 81, School of Economics, Kwansei Gakuin University.

Ohinata, M. (2015). *Zōho Boseiai shinwa no wana (Trap of Maternity Love Myth)*. Nippon Hyoron Sha: Tokyo.

Osawa, M. (2004). Pātotaimu rōdō no kokusai hikaku-kinkō shogū no genjō to shōrai-zō (International Comparison about Part-time Working-Current Situation of Balanced Treatment and Future Vision). *Business Labor Trend, 2004*(3), 2–6.

Park, S. (2008). A study on the relationship of gender equity within family and second birth. *Korea Journal of Population Studies, 31*(1), 64–71.

Presidential Committee on Aging Society and Population Policy. (2019). Change of the paradigm. Presidential committee on aging society and population policy homepage, 10 November, 2019. https://www.betterfuture.go.kr.

Sakazune, S. (2015). A study of the gap between desired and actual number of children. *Contemporary Society, 18,* 117–124.

Statistics Korea. (2016). *Local area labour force survey*.

Shigeno, Y. (2006). Syurouto syussan, ikujino ryouritsu—kigyouno ikujisiento hoikusyono syussyouritsukaihukuen o kouka (Compatibility between Employment and Childbirth/childcare—Effects of childcare support of company and nursery school on fertility recovery). In Y. Higuchi (Ed.), *Syoshikato nihonno keizaisyakai (Low Fertility and Economic Society in Japan)* (pp. 81–114). Tokyo: Nippon Hyoron Sha.

Takayama, I. (2002). Institutionalization of preschool education and the myth of first three years—An analysis using JGSS-2000 data. *JGSS Research Series, 1,* 159–169.

Van Peer, C. (2002). Desired and achieved fertility, in Klijzing. In E. M. Corjin (Ed.), *Dynamics of fertility and partnership in Europe: Insights and lessons from comparative research volumeII* (pp. 117–141). United Nations: New York and Geneva.

Woo, H. B. (2018). Population policies in the era of low fertility-current state and future directions in South Korea. *Korean Journal of Population Studies, 41*(2), 31–59.

Yamaguchi, K. (2009). *Wākuraifubaransu: Jisshō to seisaku teigen (Work-life balance: Empirical analyses and policy recommendations)*. Tokyo: Nikkei Publishing Inc.

Chapter 3
Lowest-Low Fertility in Singapore: Current State and Prospects

Keita Suga

Abstract By conducting a decomposition analysis on ethnicity-specific fertility changes since the 1970s, we show nuptiality rather than marital fertility has been the main driving force for all major ethnic groups in Singapore. Using a micro-level data, we examine first marriage timings of Singaporean youths to show (1) gender differentials in the effects of ethnicity and managerial, professional, and special first occupations, and (2) gender indifferences in the effects of birth country and extending schooling. We discuss their consequences on population structures under prevalent phenomena of international and inter-ethnic marriages in Singapore.

We explore factors affecting the current state of lowest-low fertility in Singapore to empirically seek the Singaporean prospects of population structures. We focus on ethnic diversity in Singapore society as a key aspect regulating evolution of Singaporean fertility. We also focus on rapid expansions of higher education as another key ingredient.

Our analyses combine both macro- and micro-data to strength flexibility of latter and reliability of former each other. Macro data we demonstrated are derived from *Population Census* and *Vital statistics*, both of which are known to hold highest accuracy among population statistics in Singapore. We show recent developments of fertility and nuptiality since 1970s. Specifically, we focus on ethnic differentials revealing in period fertility measures. Then, by conducting a decomposition analysis, we argue a relative importance of nuptiality's role on the fertility changes comparing with marital reproduction.

We analyze a micro-level data drawn from the 2016 survey, *Opinion Survey on Marriage, family and work*, for patterns and factors on first marriage timing of youth in contemporary Singapore. Our primary focus is gender differences in effects of extended schooling and managerial, professional, and special first occupations after the schooling on delaying first marriage. We also stress a gender difference in ethnicity effect of Non-Chinese marrying early, and a gender indifference in a birth

K. Suga (✉)
National Institute of Population and Social Security Research, Tokyo, Japan
e-mail: suga-keita@ipss.go.jp

S. Matsuda (ed.), *Low Fertility in Japan, South Korea, and Singapore*,
Population Studies of Japan, https://doi.org/10.1007/978-981-15-2830-9_3

country effect by that both of Chinese and Non-Chinese native Singaporean (who were born in the city-state) get married later than non-natives (who were born outside Singapore).

Next section reviews an ethnic stability of Singaporean youth population of past two decades and shows the census data indicating rapid expansions of higher education after the establishment of the Republic of Singapore in 1965. Section three presents a decomposition analysis on fertility changes for contributions of marital status and marital fertility. Section four accounts the method and results of the event history analysis for first marriage timing. Final section discusses implications and prospects for a population structure in Singapore. Throughout this paper, we use terms of race and ethnicity interchangeably without offense.

3.1 Brief reviews of Demographic Profiles of Singapore Youth: Ethnicity and Education

3.1.1 Population Census and Vital Statistics in Singapore

Throughout this study, we use aggregate data taken from publicized statistical tables of decennial *Census of Population*, *General Household Survey*, Annual *Report of Registration of Births and Deaths Statistics*, and *Statistics on Marriages and Divorces*.[1] All these statistics prevail high accuracy but require a caution when combined. On the one hand, the censuses counted and included only Singapore residents, that is composed of citizens and permanent residents, but excluded foreigners. In fact, we only acquire total number of foreigners but not age and sex compositions, ethnicity and marital status, etc. On the other hand, the vital statistics cover all incidences of births and deaths that were occurred in Singapore, irrespective of residential status. However, it does not report the births and deaths happened only to Singapore residents excluding those to foreigners. Hence, we only have resident populations as exposures to demographic events experienced by all populations including foreigners. This inconsistency between numerator (demographic events) and denominator (population at risk) induces an upward bias in calculation of demographic rates.

Because of intensive international migrations, the proportion of non-resident population among the total population has increased rapidly and has reached a considerable fraction after the 2000s: 5.5% (1980), 10.2% (1990), 18.7% (2000), 25.7% (2010), and 29.5% (2015). Interpretation of results for the macro analysis necessarily pertains a caution. As we discussed later, in a case of fertility, ethnicity-specific statistics for Chinese and Malay are suffered by less severe biases.

[1]See Saw (2007) for thorough explanation about population statistics in Singapore.

3.1.2 Ethnic Diversity

There are three major ethnic groups in Singapore population: Chinese, Malay, Indian, and others. The number and composition of ethnicity-specific population age 15–49 for 1960–2015 are shown in Table 3.1. The data prior to 1980 refer total population including foreigners, while the table shows Singapore residents on and after 1980 that are composed of citizens and permanent residents. The reproductive age population of all ethnic groups increased from 728.3 thousands in 1960 to 1,989.9 thousands in 2015 at an average annual growth rate of 1.8% and it has been nearly tripled in one-half century. For overall of this period, youth population of all major ethnic groups grew by a similar pace at average annual growth rates of 1.8% for Chinese and Malay and 1.9% for Indian, though Chinese and Malay's increases were slowed down after the late 1990s and Indian and Other's figures were boosted in the 2000s.

Regardless of the rise in the number, ethnic compositions of Singapore youth population have been stable over the last half century: 73–79% for Chinese, 13–14% for Malay, and 6–10% for Indian. As we will discuss shortly, fertility rates have been distinguishably higher in Malay than those of Chinese and Indian during this period, Malay proportion in live births is higher than the population composition in Table 3.1. Instead, immigrants of Chinese, Indian, and other ethnic groups are intensive and compensate for fertility differences as resulting in a stable ethnic composition for the decades. In the late 2000s, Singapore government exercised an excessive immigration adaptation policy. The policy last for a few years, however, Indian and other ethnic groups were quickly expanded, and they became to share Singapore youth population as Malay did by 2010.

3.1.3 Education Developments

Education, or human capital accumulation, is assessed to perform as an engine of Singapore's economic growth (Sun 2012: p. 56). Because of scarce natural resources, investing government budgets on human resources was one of the primary strategies for economic development. Because of page limitation, we cannot review the education system in Singapore here. (please refer Chap. 4 of this volume). But, the government efforts are reflected in a rapid increase in higher education attained by cohorts born after 1960 who started primary education in the independent Republic of Singapore. Table 3.2 shows Singaporean resident population's education attainment distribution by birth cohorts. It is calculated by a statistical table for non-student populations by age and education qualifications in *Population Census 2010*. Except for the youngest age group who were born in 1980–1985 (age 25–29 in 2010), the schooling after the census do not enhance the figures much further and should be regarded as the cohort's final status. From the table, we see that the rates of populations with some diploma and a university degree was sharply increased between cohorts born in 1955–1960 and born in 1960–1965 from 20.6 to 30.2%, and the rates of higher education were uplifted

Table 3.1 Population of age 15–49 by ethnic group in Singapore: 1960–2015

	Ethnic compositions of population (%)					Populations by ethnic group (1000)				
	Total	Malay	Chinese	Indian	Other	Total	Malay	Chinese	Indian	Other
1960	100.0	14.4	73.8	9.8	2.0	728	105	538	71	15
1965	100.0	14.2	75.9	8.2	1.7	841	120	638	69	15
1970	100.0	14.1	76.6	7.3	2.1	1015	143	777	74	21
1975	100.0	14.1	77.2	6.6	2.1	1225	173	946	81	25
1980	100.0	14.2	78.6	6.3	0.9	1322	187	1039	83	12
1985	100.0	14.0	78.4	6.7	0.9	1478	207	1158	98	14
1990	100.0	13.4	78.7	6.9	0.9	1642	221	1292	114	16
1995	100.0	13.2	78.8	7.0	1.1	1790	236	1410	125	19
2000	100.0	13.3	77.6	7.7	1.3	1878	250	1458	145	25
2005	100.0	13.8	75.4	8.7	2.1	1923	265	1451	167	41
2010	100.0	13.6	72.6	10.0	3.9	2035	276	1478	203	79
2015	100.0	13.8	72.6	9.8	3.8	1990	274	1445	196	76

Source Singapore Census of Population, 1970. Department of Statistics Singapore, "SingStat Table Builder." http://www.tablebuilder.singstat.gov.sg/ (accessed on 7th May 2018)

Note Data prior to 1980 refer to total population which include foreigners, while data from 1980 onwards refer to Singapore residents which are composed of citizens and permanent residents

Table 3.2 Singapore resident's age-specific rate of educational attainment by sex

Birth year	Highest qualification						
	Total	No qualification	Primary	Secondary	Post-secondary (non-tertiary)	Polytechnic, professional qualification, and diploma	University
Total residents							
1980–1985	100.0	0.8	1.0	14.9	11.9	25.5	45.8
1975–1980	100.0	1.4	1.7	17.1	9.6	23.1	47.2
1970–1975	100.0	2.8	2.8	22.9	12.0	19.6	39.9
1965–1970	100.0	5.8	5.1	32.3	11.9	15.8	29.0
1960–1965	100.0	9.7	8.8	41.0	10.2	11.3	18.9
1955–1960	100.0	14.9	12.3	42.0	10.2	8.9	11.7
1950–1955	100.0	19.5	13.0	43.1	8.7	6.8	8.8
1945–1950	100.0	30.0	13.1	37.4	6.9	5.6	6.9
Male							
1980–1985	100.0	0.6	0.9	15.1	15.0	26.4	42.0
1975–1980	100.0	1.1	1.5	15.9	11.1	23.4	47.1
1970–1975	100.0	2.4	2.3	20.1	12.5	19.3	43.4
1965–1970	100.0	5.9	4.5	27.1	12.4	16.3	33.8
1960–1965	100.0	9.3	8.3	36.9	10.7	12.2	22.6
1955–1960	100.0	13.2	11.7	39.5	10.5	10.5	14.6
1950–1955	100.0	14.8	11.5	43.2	9.8	9.0	11.6
1945–1950	100.0	22.3	12.5	39.8	8.3	7.4	9.7

(continued)

Table 3.2 (continued)

Birth year	Highest qualification						
	Total	No qualification	Primary	Secondary	Post-secondary (non-tertiary)	Polytechnic, professional qualification, and diploma	University
Female							
1980–1985	100.0	1.0	1.1	14.8	9.2	24.7	49.3
1975–1980	100.0	1.6	1.8	18.1	8.3	22.9	47.3
1970–1975	100.0	3.2	3.2	25.5	11.5	19.9	36.7
1965–1970	100.0	5.8	5.6	37.3	11.6	15.3	24.5
1960–1965	100.0	10.2	9.3	45.1	9.7	10.4	15.2
1955–1960	100.0	16.7	12.9	44.5	9.8	7.3	8.8
1950–1955	100.0	24.3	14.4	43.0	7.6	4.6	6.0
1945–1950	100.0	37.5	13.7	35.2	5.5	3.9	4.2

Source Singapore Census of Population, 2010. Department of Statistics Singapore

dramatically to 44.9% (1965–1970 cohort), 59.5% (1975–1980 cohort), and 70.3% (1975–1980 cohort). At the same time, four-year university education became pervasive among the higher educations: university graduates accounted for 11.7% of 1955–1960 birth cohort and comprised 47.2% of 1975–1980 cohort. Furthermore, such prevalence of higher educations occurred quickly among women than men. Among 1955–1960 birth cohort, rates of a diploma/degree holder were 25.1% of male and 16.1% of female. This rate increased to 70.5% of male and 70.1% of female born in 1975–1980. In the pre-independence era, female Singaporeans were less likely received higher education than males did, however, females acquired at least as equivalent levels of higher educations as males did in a decade.

Universality may well explain Singapore's phenomenon of rising higher education. In addition to the shrinking gender difference in the highest attainment level, Table 3.2 shows proportions without the secondary education have been virtually disappeared from both sexes' school year cohorts in the decade after the independence. In 1945–1950 birth cohort, females with primary or less educations accounted for 51.2% contrasting to male's proportion 34.9% that resulted in 16.3%-points gender difference. This gap in lower educations has been quickly diminished to 2.0%-points difference (by male 19.5% and female 17.6%) in 1960–1965 cohort. In the 1945–1950 birth cohort (age 25–29 in 1975), 37.5% of females did have no education qualifications who would likely be illiterate. This figure dropped to 5.8% by 1965–1970 birth cohort (age 25–29 in 1995). Hence, uneducated women practically vanished from the prime reproductive of age 20s during the 1980s; the fact by which family planning program delivered contraception methods successfully.

Another aspect we point out in education attainment is racial differences (table omitted due to page limitation). Generally speaking, "Other ethnic group" is the best educated, followed by Indian and Chinese, and Malay's rate of higher education is the lowest among Singapore residents. At least two ethnic differentials are acknowledged. First, with a comparison between Chinese and Malay who have no education qualification, shrinking patterns are quite similar. Second, though Malay's rates of higher education increased considerably from 8.9% (1960–1965 cohort) to 36.1% (1980–1985 cohort), Malay is still behind of other ethnic groups in 1980–1985 cohort: the rates with some diplomas and above are 78.1, 71.0 and 78.2% for Chinese, Indian, and Other, respectively.

3.2 Decomposition Analysis for Nuptiality and Marital Fertility

3.2.1 General Patterns of Fertility Changes of the Major Ethnic Groups in Singapore

Figure 3.1 shows that TFRs of all major ethnic groups achieved the replacement level by 1975. From the below replacement level, Malay TFR turned to increase in 1979 and stayed above the replacement level throughout the 1990s. However,

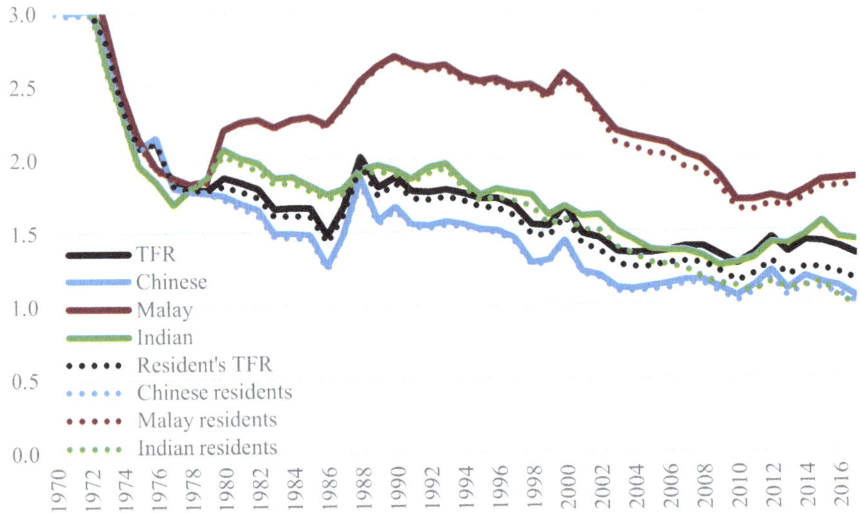

Fig. 3.1 Total fertility rate for the major ethnic group of resident population in Singapore: 1970–2017. *Source* For solid lines, Department of Statistics Singapore. "SingStat Table Builder." http://www.tablebuilder.singstat.gov.sg/ (accessed on May 2018). For a set of dot lines, calculation by author. Note: The TFRs calculated by author includes foreigner's births in the numerator, while resident populations are taken for the denominator. Ethnicity refers to those of mothers

Malay TFR is rapidly declining for 2000–2010. Chinese TFR stopped to decline in the early 1980s. It increased from 1986 to 1988 but declined steadily since the 1990s. Indian TFR increased from 1977 to recover the replacement level in 1980 but returned to follow a downward trend by slower pace than before. Indian TFR increased from 1986 to 1989 and stayed near the replacement level until 1993, however, it decreased more quickly than Chinese TFR throughout the mid-1990s and the 2000s. Nonetheless, all ethnicity-specific TFRs seem to turn to increase (at least stop declining) from 2010.

As we noted in Sect. 3.1.1, age-specific fertility rates are upward biased and so TFRs in Fig. 3.1 are, because the vital statistics report all live births occurred in Singapore while no tabulations for age-specific female foreigners are released for decomposition analysis. Singapore department of statistics calculates Singapore resident's TFR after 1980, for which foreign women's births were subtracted. On the one hand, the difference of TFR calculated here from the official resident's TFR is expanding after the 2000s. The averages of the differences are 0.042 for 1970–2000 and 0.124 for 2000–2017, and this expansion of discrepancy causes a reduction in timeseries correlation coefficients from 0.999 (1970–2000) to 0.926 (2000–2017). On the other hand, sizes of the discrepancy significantly vary by ethnicity: averages (maximums in parentheses) of differences for 1980–2017 are 0.029 (0.053), 0.038 (0.097) and 0.120 (0.434) for Chinese, Malay, and Indian, respectively. Timeseries correlation coefficients between the Singapore resident's TFR and own calculation for 2000–2017 are 0.993, 0.997, 0.673 for Chinese,

Malay, and Indian, respectively. These patterns in the discrepancy seem to be consistent with the gender- and ethnicity-specific increase of immigration which would have brought international and inter-ethnic marriages (details omitted due to page restriction but see footnotes 3–4), we should be cautious in interpretation of decomposition results especially for Indian population after the 2000s. Because the marital statuses are those of residents taken from the census data and numerators of fertility rates are inflated, marital fertility effects rather than nuptiality effects would be upward biased. Other than that, we do not suspect serious biases in the decomposition analysis as far as risks attributable to foreigner's births were concerned.

3.2.2 *Ethnic Patterns of Nuptiality by Gender*

To learn ethnic patterns of nuptiality, we focus not on marriage registrations released in the vital statistics (flow data) but on marital status surveyed in the population censuses (stock data). Because a change in the marital status distribution accounts for nuptiality in the decomposition analysis below, we transform ethnicity- and age-specific proportions of the never-married population to show Hajnal's singulate mean age at marriage (SMAM in Hajnal 1953: pp. 129–131) in Table 3.3 as a descriptive statistics to acquire insights for understanding decomposition results. It is based on the rate of Singapore citizens and permanent residents (on and after 1990) so does not suffer foreigner's marriage registrations but incorporate naturalized immigrant's marriage history outside Singapore.

Malay males and females marry earlier than Chinese males and females. Contrasting to the clear ethnic diversity of period fertility developments (Sect. 3.2.1), general tendency of delayed marriage is a common phenomenon among all ethnic groups of both sexes,[2] and these ethnic differentials preserved for 1970–2015. In 1970, marriage in Singapore was early and universal: female's SMAM was below 25 and celibacy rate by the end of her reproductive ages was less than 4%. By 1990, the never-married rates increased in all age groups of both males and females. After remaining at around same levels during the 1990s, late marriages were accelerated after 2000.

[2]There found to be an exception for Indian around year 2000 whose rates of the never married at age 20s dropped by unverifiable reasons. During the 1990–2000s, Indian immigration of age 25–44 was substantial: Indian resident's cohort change of age 5–39 to 15–49 (its ratio to cohort size at the beginning of period in parentheses) was 25,900 (28%) for 1990–2000 and 56,300 (39%) for 2000–2010, all of which were attributable to residents born outside of Singapore; proportions born outside Singapore among age 15–49 Indian residents (year in parenthesis) were 18% (1990), 29% (2000), and 47% (2010) (author's calculation based on *Census of Population, 1990, 2000, 2010*). Depending on marital status of immigrants and their marriage behavior, rate of never-married residents can change unpredictably.

Table 3.3 Singapore resident men and women's singulate mean age at marriage[a] for major ethnic groups: 1970–2015

	Female				Male			
	All	Chinese	Malay	Indian	All	Chinese	Malay	Indian
1970	24.2	24.8	22.5	22.6	27.8	28.2	26.6	26.1
1980	26.2	26.6	24.8	25.3	28.4	28.6	27.3	28.1
1990	27.0	27.6	25.2	26.4	29.9	30.4	28.2	28.3
1995	27.1	27.6	25.3	26.5	30.4	30.8	28.8	29.2
2000	26.5	27.1	25.0	24.6	30.0	30.3	28.8	29.0
2005	26.9	27.6	25.3	24.3	30.1	30.5	29.8	28.5
2010	27.9	28.7	26.8	24.9	30.4	31.0	30.0	28.9
2015	28.7	29.3	27.8	26.7	30.9	31.3	30.2	30.1

Source Author's calculation based on age specific rate of the never-married population by age in *Singapore Census of Population*, 1970–1990, 2000, 2010. *General Household Survey*, 1995, 2005, 2015. Data prior to 1990 refer to total population which include foreigners, while data from 1990 onwards refer to Singapore residents which are composed of citizens and permanent residents. Marital status was collected by sampling surveys in both of the censuses and GHS. The size of sample varies by survey year ranging from 20% for 1980–2000 to 3% in 2015
Notes [a]Singulate Mean Age at Marriage is calculated by $\Sigma(15 + S_x - 50 * S_{50})/(1 - S_{50})$, where S_x refers the rate of the never-married population at age x and the summation is taken over all reproductive ages

Despite the general tendency of late marriage among ethnic groups, the extent of the delays differs between genders. Annual average growth rates of SMAMs show steeper rises for females: 0.78% (1970–1980), 0.06% (1980–2000), and 0.53% (2000–2015); 0.36% (1970–1990), 0.03% (1990–2000), and 0.21% (2000–2015) for males. Although not shown in the table, further examination on the age-specific rates reveals that there was a surge between 1975 and 1980 birth cohort and younger (age 25–29 and below in 2005) from the former cohorts. These sudden rises were common among Chinese and Malay of both sexes but substantial among females: Chinese and Malay female's never-married rates of age 25–29 increased by 23.6%-points (from 44.5 to 68.0%) and 25.7%-points (from 25.6 to 51.3%) during 2000–2015, respectively; Male's rises for the same period were 16.3%-points (from 66.5% to 82.8%) and 15.4%-points (from 53.5% to 68.9%) for Chinese and Malay, respectively. Because of female's faster extensions in the never-married life, gender differences in the average age at marriage shrunk from 3.3 years (in 2000) and 4.5 years (in 2005) to 2.0 years and 2.4 years in 2015 for Chinese and Malay, respectively. It is interesting to notice that regardless of these age differentials between husbands and wives revealed in SMAM (husbands on average marring late by about three years), the never-married rates of age 45–49 were lower in male than those in female after the mid-1990s. These gender differences could be caused by intensive expansion of international and inter-ethnic marriage, in which proportion of foreign wife is double that of foreign husband.[3]

3.2.3 A Simple Decomposition Method Suitable for Singapore

We would like to decompose the changes of the period TFRs into contributions of nuptiality and marital fertility. Seeking the simplest possible way, we apply a basic method, two-factor case for the rate as the product of factors (Das Gupta 1993: pp. 6–7). TFRs can be expressed in Eq. 3.1:

$$\mathrm{TFR} = \sum_{x=15-19}^{45-49} \left(\frac{B_x^{\mathrm{CM}}}{F_x^{\mathrm{CM}}} \frac{F_x^{\mathrm{CM}}}{F_x} + \frac{B_x^{\mathrm{UM}}}{F_x^{UM}} \frac{F_x^{\mathrm{UM}}}{F_x} \right) \quad (3.1)$$

where $F_x = F_x^{\mathrm{CM}} + F_x^{\mathrm{UM}}$, F_x^{CM} denotes age-specific currently married female population of age x, F_x^{UM} refers to those not currently married, and $\{B_x^{\mathrm{CM}}, B_x^{\mathrm{UM}}\}$ stands for births given by age x mother of corresponding marital status. To simplify the notation, we suppress ethnicity of mothers, however, Eq. 3.1 is calculated by ethnicity.

Equation 3.1 requires unavailable birth data disassembled by marital status of mother. However, under the strong norm of East Asian family tradition, childbearing and marriage are firmly tied especially in Chinese society. The percentage out-of-wedlock birth rates in Singapore during the 1990s–2010s accounted for around 1% (*the Report on the Registration of Births and Deaths Statistics, 2001,* and later). In addition, the out-of-wedlock birth rates do not show evident increasing or decreasing tendency for all ethnicity. We safely assume that the contribution of *change* in unmarried woman's birth (B_x^{UM}/F_x) is negligible to period fertility changes and that ratios of illegitimate births to currently married women are unchanged over the analysis period. By these two assumptions, Eq. 3.1 reduces to Eq. 3.2 which decompose s-year change of the period TFRs into two components:

---

[3]According to Singapore Department of Statistics (http://www.tablebuilder.singstat.gov.sg/publicfacing/mainMenu.action/ access on 11th November 2018), among marriages registered in Singapore during 1985–1990, residential status of husband and wife was composed of marriages 85.4% between resident husband and resident wife, 9.2% resident husband and non-resident wife, 3.9% non-resident husband and resident wife, and 1.5% non-resident spouses, implying that non-resident rates were 5.4% of husbands and 10.7% of wives. The non-resident rates of both spouses grew substantially: 7.0% (1995–2000) and 15.5% (2010–2015) for husbands; 21.2% (1995–2000) and 30.6% (2010–2015) for wives.

$$
\begin{aligned}
&\mathrm{TFR}(t) - \mathrm{TFR}(t-s) \\
&= \sum_{x=15-19}^{45-49} \left(\frac{B_x(t)}{F_x^{\mathrm{CM}}(t)} - \frac{B_x(t-s)}{F_x^{\mathrm{CM}}(t-s)} \right) \left(\frac{F_x^{\mathrm{CM}}(t)}{F_x(t)} + \frac{F_x^{\mathrm{CM}}(t-s)}{F_x(t-s)} \right) /2 \\
&+ \sum_{x=15-19}^{45-49} \left(\frac{B_x(t)}{F_x^{\mathrm{CM}}(t)} + \frac{B_x(t-s)}{F_x^{\mathrm{CM}}(t-s)} \right) \left(\frac{F_x^{\mathrm{CM}}(t)}{F_x(t)} - \frac{F_x^{\mathrm{CM}}(t-s)}{F_x(t-s)} \right) /2
\end{aligned} \tag{3.2}
$$

The first term corresponds with the contribution of marital fertility rates and the second term quantifies the contribution of currently married rates.

3.2.4 Decomposition Results: Ethnic Similarities and Differentials in Momentous Role of Nuptiality

There are ethnic similarities and differentials in nuptiality and marital fertility effects on period fertility changes in Singapore. Following the fall in the 1970s (and in the early 1980s for Chinese and Indian), TFRs of all major ethnic groups recovered in the late-1980s. Throughout the 1990s and the 2000s, the TFRs declined consistently. For 1990–2015 overall, late and less marriages account for all the fall of all major ethnic groups in Singapore (Table 3.4). Moreover, if no change in nuptiality was occurred, marital fertility rates would make TFRs 20–30% higher. In fact, nuptiality effects lowered TFRs in all decennial (and quinquennial) periods during the 1970–2010 (and 1990–2015) of all major ethnic groups, except for the Indian late-1990s (detailed results omitted due to page restriction). Nuptiality is an essential determinant for lowest-low fertility in Singaporean ethnic societies.

Detailed examinations by period reveal ethnic differentials in the nuptial and marital fertility effects on TFRs. In the 1970s, both nuptiality and marital fertility effects reduced TFRs of all major ethnic groups, however, the sizes differed: delaying marriage affected instrumentally for Indian, while limiting numbers of children among married couples lowed TFRs more in Chinese and Malay. In the 1980s, marital fertility effects turned to positive and nuptiality effects continued to be negative for all major ethnic groups, but again sizes differed: Malay TFR recovered above the replacement level as a result of substantial gains from marital fertility; Chinese and Indian marital fertility effects were positive but dominated by depressing marriage effects. In the 1990s, the marital fertility effect continued to be positive for Malay but became negative for Chinese and Indian. In this period, the marital fertility effect dominated in the TFR declines for Chinese and Indian, Chinese TFR decreased due both to nuptiality and marital fertility, while marital fertility effect completely explained Indian's decline and nuptiality effect totally

Table 3.4 Decompositions for changes in TFRs into contributions of marital fertility and nuptiality for the major ethnic group in Singapore

Ethnic group	Period	TFR		Change in	Contributions of changes in		Percent distributions	
		Begin	End	TFR (End–Begin)	Marital fertility	% Married	Marital fertility	% Married
Chinese	1970–1980	3.136	1.758	−1.378	−0.983	−0.395	−71.3	−28.7
	1980–1990	1.758	1.674	−0.084	0.155	−0.239	185.9	−285.9
	1990–2000	1.674	1.449	−0.225	−0.155	−0.070	−68.8	−31.2
	2000–2010	1.449	1.054	−0.395	−0.061	−0.334	−15.4	−84.6
	2010–2015	1.054	1.144	0.089	0.198	−0.108	221.2	−121.2
	1990–2015	1.674	1.144	−0.530	0.110	−0.641	20.8	−120.8
Malay	1970–1980	3.774	2.199	−1.575	−0.936	−0.639	−59.4	−40.6
	1980–1990	2.199	2.704	0.505	0.603	−0.099	119.6	−19.6
	1990–2000	2.704	2.583	−0.121	0.111	−0.231	91.4	−191.4
	2000–2010	2.583	1.714	−0.869	−0.183	−0.686	−21.1	−78.9
	2010–2015	1.714	1.842	0.128	0.320	−0.192	249.9	−149.9
	1990–2015	2.704	1.842	−0.862	0.256	−1.118	29.7	−129.7
Indian	1970–1980	3.354	2.077	−1.278	−0.475	−0.803	−37.2	−62.8
	1980–1990	2.077	1.929	−0.148	0.047	−0.195	31.8	−131.8
	1990–2000	1.929	1.680	−0.249	−0.398	0.149	−160.0	60.0
	2000–2010	1.680	1.282	−0.398	−0.213	−0.185	−53.5	−46.5
	2010–2015	1.282	1.567	0.285	0.600	−0.315	210.6	−110.6
	1990–2015	1.929	1.567	−0.361	0.078	−0.439	21.5	−121.5

Source Author's calculation based on age-specific fertility rates summarized in Fig. 3.1 and marital status used for Table 3.3

accounted for Malay's decline. For the 2000s, marital fertility effects became negative again for all three major ethnic groups. More importantly, the negative nuptiality effects were reinforced for all, though relative importance of the two effects differentiated: nuptiality was the main reason for Chinese and Malay; marital reproduction was relatively important for Indian.[4] In the early-2010s, marital fertility recovery was in common with steady nuptiality declines for all major ethnic groups. We must cautiously assess Indian results after the late 1990s, however, it should not ruin the fact that after the 1990s nuptiality was main driving force for TFR declines of all major ethnic groups with enforcing its power in the 2000s.

[4]Indian age-specific fertility rates used for analysis were upward biased due to foreigner's births but marital status data did not contain such discrepancies, if ignoring consequences of immigration (see footnote 3). Negative marital fertility effects were likely estimated larger than the reality (though the immigration complicates the direction of both effects).

3.3 Event History Analysis for First Marriage Timing

3.3.1 Methodology and Work Data

We analyze the micro-data from the Opinion Survey on Marriage, Family, and Work (2016OSMFW hereafter). Conducted in February–March 2016 via computer-assisted face-to-face interview, 2016OSMFW is a national representative sample of 800 men and women aged 20–49 of all marital statuses who lived in Singapore. The survey covered three of the four major official languages in Singapore: English, Chinese, and Malay.

Sampling of 2016OSMFW initially set simply randomly selected 800 addresses over the city-state. If the interview in a selected point was not successful, the survey in another location was conducted for an address apart from a pre-specified interval in the list.[5] So, our sampling scheme entitled was a household sampling not a population sampling. Total of 803 usable questionnaires was collected and the response rate was 56.2%. Preliminary analysis for the representativeness of the sample shows in general good properties in terms of the age-sex distribution and the ethnic compositions by age or sex. With excluding 22 cases whose years of first marriage were unknown, work data include 781 Singapore residents (citizens and permanent residents) of all marital statuses.

We first conduct the Cox proportional hazard analysis (Cox 1972) on first marriage occurrences separately by genders.[6] Then, to test possible gender differences in the effects of covariates on first marriage timing, we pool male and female data and estimate models with adding one by one of demographic and socio-economic covariates with interactions to a dichotomous indicator for gender. In this pooled model, we specify baseline hazards stratified by genders, which is equivalent to fitting a separate relative risk model by genders under the constraint that the coefficients are equal while the baseline hazard functions are not. This specification formally tests gender differences in covariate's effects by allowing gender differences in the baseline hazards identified non-parametrically in the relative risk model framework.[7]

---

[5]Interview in the new candidate location was permitted if the living arrangement was similar to the initially sampled household. Only one respondent per one household was allowed to be interviewed.

[6]The Cox proportional hazard model specifies the hazard function by $h(t|x_i) = h_0(t)\exp(x_i\beta)$ where $h_0(t)$ denotes the baseline hazard function of analysis time t, x_i expresses a covariate multiplied by a fixed parameter (i.e., covariate's effect is proportional to the baseline). exp (β) is called hazard ratio of a (dichotomous) covariate x, because the hazard associating with the covariate is exp (β)-times bigger than the baseline hazard. Note that the baseline (reference) group should be deliberately chosen as is defined in the model by all covariates being zero.

[7]Stratified proportional hazard model by genders can be written mathematically in $h(t|x_i) = \left[h_{0,m}(t)\exp(x_i\beta)\right]^{S_i} \cdot \left[h_{0,f}(t)\exp(x_i\beta)\right]^{1-S_i}$, where S_i takes one for male and zero otherwise, $h_{0,m}(t)$ and $h_{0,f}(t)$ refer baseline hazards for male and female, respectively. Including an interaction term to gender in the model $h(t|x_i) = \left[h_{0,m}(t)\exp(x_i\beta + S_i x_i\gamma)\right]^{S_i} \cdot \left[h_{0,f}(t)\exp(x_i\beta + S_i x_i\gamma)\right]^{1-S_i}$

The Cox proportional hazard model analysis which assumes a time-fixed coefficient, TFC, well established popularity by at least twofold: (1) summarizing covariate's effects in one single measure, the hazard ratio, and (2) flexibility by unspecified shapes of the baseline hazard curve over analysis time. However, the virtue mirrors limitations: (1) the hazard ratio can be seriously biased reporting a misleading result, and (2) inability to predict hazard schedules by covariates. To cope with these, we incorporate time-varying coefficients (TVC) into the models.[8] Specifically, we include covariates and their interactions with linear analysis time. In this TVC models, total effects of a covariate are composed sum of time-fixed parameter (main effect of the covariate that is constant over analysis time and proportionally lifts up/down baseline hazard functions) and time-varying parameter (interaction effect with analysis time that accounts for the change of the main effect as analysis time pasts). In order to improve comparability between estimation results by genders and of male and female pooled data, analysis time was centered at mean years of failure times by genders (28.6 for male; 26.2 for female) before taking interactions.[9] The change of coefficient as analysis time proceeds is hard to conceive by parameter estimates, so we report hazard ratios predicted by parameter estimates for several points in analysis time.

In the estimation, population at risk is the never-married males and females. The analysis time is age (measured in months). In macro analysis, we found the salient differentials in marriage timing by ethnic group under increasing phenomena of international and inter-ethnic marriage. In Singapore, never-married males and females can legally marry from age 16 or from age 18 according to their race[10]. This difference in the marriage institution may regulate the length of duration under the marriage risk, with depending on an extent of an infrequent immigration after

implies the following hazard functions: $h_{0,m}(t)\exp(x_i(\beta+\gamma))$ for male; $h_{0,f}(t)\exp(x_i\beta)$ for female. Then, gender differences in covariate's effects can be easily tested by $\gamma = 0$.

[8]A time-varying coefficient is a way to deal with non-proportionality. The specification works in bringing a time scale into the model. Note that the Cox proportional hazard with time-fixed coefficient model is identified only by the order of event occurrences (e.g., for the Cox model $h_0(t)\exp(x_i\beta)$ in footnote 7, any increasing transformation $f(\cdot)$ of analysis time (as long as independent of covariates) gives the same parameter estimates as in $h(f(t)|x_i) = h_0(f(t))\exp(x_i\beta)$ where $h_0(\cdot)$ denotes the baseline hazard).

[9]Our TVC models is expressed mathematically in $h(t|x_i) = \left[h_{0,m}(t)\exp(x_i(\beta+\theta(t-\mu_m)) + S_i x_i(\gamma+\lambda(t-\mu_m)))\right]^{S_i} \cdot \left[h_{0,f}(t)\exp\left(x_i\left(\beta+\theta\left(t-\mu_f\right)\right)\right)\right]^{1-S_i}$, where the same notation is employed as those in footnote 8, in addition to that $\{\theta, \lambda\}$ are fixed parameters and $\{\mu_m, \mu_f\}$ refer to mean years of analysis time only when some subjects fail. The statistical significance of a covariate's effects and its gender difference is jointly tested by $\{\beta, \theta\} = 0$ for males and females and $\{\gamma, \lambda\} = 0$, respectively.

[10]The Muslim Marriage Act permits to marry from age 16, while the Women's Charter prohibits a marriage of age under 18.

the age beginning the risk.[11] We incorporate delayed entry in the estimation (i.e., subjects become at risk for first marriage from age 16 or 18 by depending on their races). Additionally, in all estimation models, we decided to include demographic covariates: dichotomous indicators of Non-Chinese and birth country whether born outside Singapore, together with birth cohort (minus 1980).

Socio-economic factors include (1) respondent's education attainment and (2) a dichotomous indicator for managerial, professional, and special first occupations after schooling. In 2016OSMFW, education attainment was collected by category (No formal education, GCE 'O' level or below, GCE 'A' level, Diploma, University or above). Because preliminary analysis shows equally consistent predictions for survival probability of higher education categories by linearity restriction and its gains in efficiency, we transform the categorical variable to a continuous schooling years (by assuming six years, ten years, twelve years, thirteen years, and sixteen years in the same order appeared in the previous parentheses) then subtract mean years (13.3) to set the baseline hazard for sensible interpretations.

3.3.2 Descriptive Analysis

In Table 3.5, we made a simple tabulation for mean ages at first marriage and percentages ever-married males and females by demographic and socio-economic covariates. Stars in the table indicate significance levels of a covariate by testing null hypothesis that difference of the covariate-specific means from overall means by genders equals to zero. Needless to say, respondents who were never married at the time of the survey did not know the age at first marriage. We were able to make simple tabulations only for ever-married respondents.

In general, we expect higher rates of never-married associating with late marriages or higher ages at first marriage. However, when a significant portion of population was never-married (i.e., right censored), estimates of mean age at first marriage only with ever-married (by a certain upper boundary age) would suffer from severe downward biases. It is not recommended that we argue marriage timing among population sub-groups solely based on the mean age at first marriage. Here, we descriptively tabulate our dependent variable to acquire a sense about work data, based on which we proceed to event history analysis to cope with such biases.

Table 3.5 shows that two third of females had ever married at least once, while only slightly more than half males did so by the time of survey, which resulted in

[11]We do not know when immigrating to Singapore if respondents born outside Singapore. It prohibits controlling the duration under risk onset of being in Singapore. Yet we measure an average risk ratio of immigrants relative to those born-in and grown-up. The difference in age beginning the risk could cause a non-proportionality in hazard functions by ethnicity and birth country. However, non-parametric identification of hazards seems unfeasible with given limited size of cases. Rather, we test a significance of time-varying coefficients to report the 'average' risk ratios over time as quantifying and highlighting the effect.

Table 3.5 Rate of the ever-married and mean age at 1st marriage by demographic and socio-economic characteristics, accompanying with tests for the significance by gender: Singaporean of age 20–49 in 2016

	Mean age at 1st marriage			Rate of the ever-married (%)			Total number of cases[a]		
	Total	Male	Female	Total	Male	Female	Total	Male	Female
Total	27.1–	28.6***	26.2***	60.2–	52.1***	65.6***	781	313	468
Born in Singapore	26.7*	28.4	25.8*	49.1***	42.6***	54.0***	550	235	315
Born outside Singapore	27.5*	29.1	26.7*	86.6***	80.8***	89.5***	231	78	153
Chinese	27.6***	28.9	27.0***	55.5***	47.0**	60.5***	539	200	339
Malay, Indian and Other	26.1***	28.3	24.7***	70.7***	61.1**	79.1***	242	113	129
Respondent's education									
University graduates	28.5***	29.6***	27.8***	62.9	64.7***	61.8	310	119	191
Other educational attainment	26.0***	27.8***	25.2***	58.4	44.3***	68.2	471	194	277
Occupation of 1st job									
Manager, Professional and Specialist	28.2***	29.0	27.5***	67.9***	66.7***	68.9	249	117	132
Other occupation	26.4***	28.4	25.7***	56.6***	43.4***	64.3	532	196	336

Note Tabulation by author. Stars indicate statistical significance at ***1% level, **5% level, *10% level under the null hypothesis: difference from gender-specific means (28.6 for males, 26.2 for females, and 27.1 overall for mean age at 1st marriage; 52.1% for males, 65.6% for females, and 60.2% overall for ever-married rates) equals to zero

[a]Exclude 22 cases (7 males and 15 females) of unknown age at 1st marriage

the 13.5%-points difference in the never-married rates between genders. Moreover, male's mean age at first marriage was 28.6 years, while it was 26.2 for female resulting in two-and-a-half-year difference which was statistically significant at 1% level. Regarding other covariates overall of both sexes, we see that Chinese married later in terms both the never-married rate and the mean age at first marriage consistently. The late marriages of Chinese males and females are consistent with findings based on the census data. However, we should pay attentions to that Chinese never-married rates is slightly larger than one half, the disparities in mean ages would expand more than those in the table, if they finally married later in their life course. Contrarily, Table 3.5 also indicates that respondents born in Singapore and those whose first occupation were managerial, professional, and special married earlier on average (in terms of the mean ages of first marriage) associating with higher never-married rates. In these cases, disparities in the mean age would be reduced or the order among birth countries and first occupations would be possibly reversed.

When looking at the table by gender, we see that Chinese females married late in terms both the mean age at first marriage and the never-married rate, the results consistent with observation for overall males and females. Because of smaller tabulation cases by gender, results for other covariates showed discrepancies: focusing on male's birth place, race and the occupation for instance, the never-married rates were statistically significantly different between population sub-groups, while mean ages at first marriage were not statistically significant for the same sub-groups (vice versa for female's education and occupation); the never-married rate of females born in Singapore was higher than those born outside Singapore, while Singapore origin females' mean age at first marriage was lower than their counterpart.

3.3.3 The Cox Proportional Hazard Analysis by Gender

Table 3.6 shows the hazard ratios (HRs) of demographic and socio-economic covariates in the relative risk models for first marriage timing of Singaporean males and females age 20–49 in 2016. Estimated separately by gender, it shows how large the hazard rates of population sub-groups are on average through analysis time with a comparison to the gender-specific reference group(s). Time-fixed coefficient (TFC) specification model M1-0 in Table 3.6a shows statistically significant demographic effects at least 5% level for females: first marriage hazard at each age of women born outside Singapore were on average 29% larger than the reference group of those who were Chinese born in 1980 Singapore; Malay, Indian, and Other female's first marriage hazard was nearly twice as large as those of Chinese born in 1980 Singapore. The time-varying coefficient (TVC) models M1-1–M1-2 report that these demographic effects are statistically significant and time-dependent: the hazard rates of women born outside Singapore increase more rapidly over their life courses and their hazard rates become higher than those born

Table 3.6 Hazard ratios of relative risk model estimates for first marriage timing: Singaporean age 20–49 in 2016

(a) Female

	M1-0	M1-1	M1-2	M1-3	M1-4	M1-5	M1-6	M1-7
Time proportional								
Born outside Singapore (= 1)	1.290**	1.288**	1.307**	1.372***	1.395***	1.337**	1.352**	1.438***
Ethnic group								
Malay, Indian and other	1.904***	1.894***	1.782***	1.814***	1.818**	1.933***	1.935***	1.707***
Chinese[a]								
Completed years of schooling[b]				0.906***	0.916***			0.929***
1st Occupation								
Manager, professional and specialist						0.689***	0.664***	0.822
Other occupations								
Birth year—1980	0.971***	0.971***	0.973***	0.981***	0.983*	0.972***	0.973***	0.982**
Time-varing[c]								
Born outside Singapore (= 1)		1.066**						1.060*
Malay, Indian and other (= 1)			0.901***					0.903***
Completed years of schooling[b]					1.030***			1.027***
Special 1st Occupation (= 1)							1.080***	1.010
#Subjects	468	468	468	468	468	468	468	468
Person-years at risk	5143.3	5143.3	5143.3	5143.3	5143.3	5143.3	5143.3	5143.3
Log likelihood	−1601.9	−1599.4	−1597.1	−1591.8	−1576.8	−1597.4	−1594.4	−1570.0
Chi-squared stat.	41.3	43.2	53.7	51.1	96.8	40.6	49.2	112.6
AIC	3209.8	3206.8	3202.1	3191.6	3163.5	3202.8	3198.7	3157.9

(continued)

Table 3.6 (continued)

(a) Female								
	M1-0	M1-1	M1-2	M1-3	M1-4	M1-5	M1-6	M1-7
Joint test on H0: Time proportional coef. = 0 and time-varying coef. = 0								
Chi-squared stat.		10.9	33.4		51.9		15.0	
P-value		0.004	0.000		0.000		0.001	
(b) Male								
	M2-0	M2-1	M2-2	M2-3	M2-4	M2-5	M2-6	M2-7
Time proportional								
Born outside Singapore (= 1)	1.438**	1.432*	1.438**	1.516**	1.514***	1.418*	1.470**	1.559**
Ethnic group								
Malay, Indian and other	1.338	1.347	1.343	1.327	1.347	1.333	1.325	1.286
Chinese[a]								
Completed years of schooling[b]				0.971	0.964			0.941*
1st occupation								
Manager, professional and specialist						1.085	1.077	1.327
Other occupations[a]								
Birth year—1980	0.989	0.987	0.989	0.990	0.990	0.989	0.988	0.989
Time-varing[c]								
Born outside Singapore (= 1)		1.092**						1.092**
Malay, Indian and other (= 1)			1.012					0.995
Completed years of schooling[b]					1.017***			1.011
Special 1st occupation (= 1)							1.068*	1.046
#Subjects	313	313	313	313	313	313	313	313
Person-years at risk	3840.2	3840.2	3840.2	3840.2	3840.2	3840.2	3840.2	3840.2
Log likelihood	−766.6	−764.1	−766.6	−766.1	−762.4	−766.5	−764.9	−759.3
Chi-squared stat.	20.9	27.0	21.4	21.2	29.8	21.9	24.8	38.5

(continued)

Table 3.6 (continued)

(b) Male

	M2-0	M2-1	M2-2	M2-3	M2-4	M2-5	M2-6	M2-7
AIC	1539.2	1536.2	1541.1	1540.2	1534.7	1541.0	1539.8	1536.5
Joint test on H0: Time proportional coef. = 0 and time-varying coef. = 0								
Chi-squared stat.		8.8	2.6		7.4		3.7	
P-value		0.012	0.274		0.025		0.158	

Source Calculation by author
Note Statistically significant at ***1% level, **5% level, *10% level, based on standard error clustered by subjects
[a]Reference category
[b]Difference from sample mean (= 13.3) of all subjects
[c]Interactions with analysis time, which was centered at means of failure times by gender (28.6 for male; 26.2 for female) before taking interactions

in Singapore from the early 20s (threshold age = 22.3)[12]; Malay and other's hazard rates become smaller later in their life course and their hazard rates go below Chinese hazard rates from their early 30s (threshold age = 31.7). Note carefully that the table shows the HRs relative to reference groups whose hazard rates exhibit reverse-U shape with peak ages in the late 20s, so the hazard rates of Malay and other women increase in the early 20s by a slower pace than the baseline does.

Table 3.6a (M1-3–M1-6) also shows that, with demographic covariates held fixed, higher education and managerial, professional, and special first occupation cause female marriage delayed whose effects are time dependent and statistically significant at 1% level. In particular, the longer the schooling years than the average years, the higher the hazard rates after the age 30s, while lower education encourages marriages in the 20s and discourages marriages after the 30s (threshold age = 29.2), and special first occupations lower marriages in the 20s and accelerate those in the 30s and later (threshold age = 31.6). Average schooling years (13.3) of our sample corresponds a little longer than those obtained some diplomas, so females, whose marriages are delayed in comparison to the average schooling are university graduates, and with demographic covariates held fixed their HRs changes similarly to those special first occupations: HRs of sixteen-years education at exact ages 20, 30, and 40 are 0.48, 1.07, and 2.34, while they are 0.41, 0.89, and 1.91 for first special occupations. Because schooling years fit data better than the first occupations, the latter covariate loses statistical significance when putting them together (Table 3.6a M1-7). Despite being ready for instantaneous interpretation, because the effects of higher education and the special occupations are time dependent, the average HRs quantified by the TFC specifications should be viewed with a skepticism.

Generally speaking, the models for male Singaporeans show qualitatively similar effects of covariates as in female's results (Table 3.6b). However, because of relatively limited size of usable cases, male's models do not detect the statistical significance of covariate's effects except the birth country and the schooling years, both of which are time dependent. Male immigrants and highly educated males marry later in their life courses: the hazard rates of male born outside Singapore exceed those of Chinese born in Singapore 1980 after the mid-20s (threshold age = 24.5 in M2-1); the hazard rates of male university graduates are smaller than the baseline in the 20s but become higher in the 30s and later (threshold age = 30.8 in M2-4). Two remarks might attract an interest. One is that preliminary analysis found a statistically significant accelerating effect of Malay and other ethnic male, however, the ethnic effect became insignificant once the birth country effect was

[12]Table 3.6a (M1-1) indicates that the hazard rate of women born outside Singapore changes as h_0 (age) exp (b_1 + b_2 age) where h_0 (age) is the baseline hazard (of Chinese women born in 1980 Singapore), exp (b_1) = 0.240 and exp (b_2) = 1.066 constitute hazard ratios of time-fixed and time-varying parts, respectively. The hazard ratio exp (b_1 + b_2 age) equals to 1 when age = 22.3 (threshold age). This means that hazard rate of women born outside Singapore is, with other covariates controlled for, larger than the baseline before age 22 but smaller than the baseline after the age.

controlled for. Second, although it is statistically insignificant by conventional levels, male's special first occupation associates with higher hazard rates over their life course (in the TFC specification) while the special occupation effect delays female's first marriage. These estimation results imply relatively stronger accelerating effect of special first occupation for males than one for females. Further examinations uncovered that male's survival probabilities predicted by the first occupations were little different in his 20s and predicted never-married probabilities for male specialist in his mid-30s were lower than those of other occupations (i.e., more male specialists had married by the 30s than male non-specialists), while relatively large differences between first occupations, by which more female specialists being never-married, were predicted in her 20s and the decelerating first special occupation effect for females persists after the mid-30s.

3.3.4 Gender Differences and Similarities in the Demographic and Socio-economic Effects

Table 3.7 presents the HRs estimated by male and female pooled models that are consistent with models in Table 3.6. The table conducts statistical tests for the significance of gender differences in the effects of covariates. We found four statistically significant gender differences by conventional levels: TVC effects of ethnicity, TFC effects of higher education and special first occupations, and TVC effects of the special first occupations. When time-dependent characteristics of the education are modeled, the set of coefficient estimates looks qualitatively like first occupations. However, when putting all covariates together in M3-7, the gender differences in TVC ethnicity and special first occupation effects hold marginal significance (p-values are 0.065 and 0.099, respectively; not shown in the table) but the significance of TVC education effects does not remain (p value = 0.217).

By showing predicted HRs by ethnicity, schooling years, and special first occupation at exact ages 20–40, Table 3.8 elaborates these effects. The table shows the HRs predicted by M3-7 (in Table 3.7) that are the ratios relative to baseline age schedules of first marriage hazard. Since the baselines are stratified by genders, the reference groups correspond with male or female Chinese born in Singapore 1980 with average years of schooling and whose first occupation was other than manager, professional, and specialist. Note that the baseline hazard profiles are gender-specific and differ in their levels and shapes by genders, even when the HRs of both genders coincide.

The hazard rates of Malay, Indian and other ethnic males are higher over their life courses than the baseline, while the hazard rates of Non-Chinese females are larger in the 20s but lower after the early 30s than those of female Chinese born in Singapore 1980. Although the effects of schooling years are little steeper among females, the university education of both males and females suppresses marriages by the age 20s and stimulates those of the 30s and later, in comparisons with the

Table 3.7 Hazard ratio estimates of the relative model stratified baseline by gender for first marriage timing: Singapore men and women of age 20–49 in 2016

	M3-0	M3-1	M3-2	M3-3	M3-4	M3-5	M3-6	M3-7
Main								
Time proportional								
Born outside Singapore (= 1)	1.293**	1.315***	1.339***	1.390***	1.407***	1.335***	1.359***	1.440***
Ethnic group								
Malay, Indian and other	1.886***	1.674***	1.759***	1.620***	1.632***	1.683***	1.685***	1.699***
Chinese[a]								
Completed years of schooling[b]				0.903***	0.913***			0.928***
1st occupation								
Manager, professional and specialist						0.693***	0.668***	0.823
Other occupations[a]								
Birth year—1980	0.977***	0.976***	0.978***	0.985**	0.986**	0.978***	0.978***	0.985**
Time-varing[c]								
Born outside Singapore (= 1)		1.066**						1.059*
Malay, Indian and other (= 1)			0.899***					0.903***
Completed years of schooling[b]					1.030***			1.027***
Special 1st occupation (= 1)							1.080***	1.011
Interaction with Male (= 1)								
Time proportional								
Born outside Singapore (= 1)	1.086	0.980						1.072
Malay, Indian and other (= 1)	0.708		0.777					0.757
Completed years of schooling[b]				1.078**	1.057*			1.016
Special 1st occupation (= 1)						1.534**	1.586**	1.606**

(continued)

Table 3.7 (continued)

	M3-0	M3-1	M3-2	M3-3	M3-4	M3-5	M3-6	M3-7
Time-varing[c]								
Born outside Singapore (= 1)		1.028						1.032
Malay, Indian and other (= 1)			1.125**					1.100*
Completed years of schooling[b]					0.988			0.984*
Special 1st occupation (= 1)							0.990	1.036
#Subjects	781	781	781	781	781	781	781	781
Person-years at risk	8983.5	8983.5	8983.5	8983.5	8983.5	8983.5	8983.5	8983.5
Log likelihood	−2369.2	−2365.2	−2364.2	−2359.1	−2340.2	−2366.0	−2361.3	−2329.3
Chi-squared stat.	62.0	70.7	73.2	72.0	125.3	61.5	71.6	151.0
AIC	4748.4	4742.5	4740.5	4728.3	4694.4	4742.0	4736.7	4692.7
Joint test on H0: All gender-interaction coefficient = 0								
Chi-squared stat.	2.4	0.4	6.6	4.2	4.5	4.8	5.3	15.8
P-value	0.299	0.836	0.037	0.040	0.106	0.028	0.072	0.045

Source Calculation by author
Note Statistically significant at ***1% level, **5% level, *10% level, based on standard error clustered by subjects
[a]Reference category
[b]Difference from sample mean (= 13.3) of all subjects
[c]Interactions with analysis time, which was centered at means of failure times by gender (28.6 for male; 26.2 for female) before taking interactions

Table 3.8 Model predicted hazard ratios of ethnicity, schooling years and first special occupation by age and sex for first marriage timing: Singapore men and women of age 20–49 in 2016

Age	Malay, Indian, and other	Years of schooling			1st special occupation
		6 years (primary)	10 years (secondary)	16 years (university)	
Male					
20	1.36	3.03	1.65	0.66	0.89
25	1.31	2.05	1.38	0.77	1.12
30	1.28	1.38	1.16	0.89	1.41
35	1.24	0.94	0.97	1.03	1.77
40	1.20	0.63	0.81	1.19	2.22
Female					
20	3.20	5.85	2.22	0.52	0.77
25	1.92	2.20	1.43	0.75	0.81
30	1.16	0.82	0.92	1.07	0.86
35	0.69	0.31	0.59	1.55	0.90
40	0.42	0.12	0.38	2.22	0.95

Source Calculation by author
Note Hazard ratios are relative to reference groups: Chinese, average years of schooling (= 13.3), and first occupations other than those managerial, professional, and special. HRs are predicted by estimates of M3-7 (in Table 3.7)

gender-specific baseline hazards. Finally, the hazard rates of female specialists are lower over their life courses than the baseline hazard rates, while male specialist's hazard rates after the mid-20s exceed those of other first occupations.

These results conclude that in the class of TVC models the ethnicity and special first occupation effects, that quantify how the Chinese and specialists delay their marriage, are gender specific. At the same time, extensions in schooling years beyond the average years decelerate marriage timings similarly for males and females (time-dependent effects indistinguishable between genders).

3.4 Future Prospects and Concluding Remarks

By the event history analysis with using 2016OSMFW, we found a statistically significant gender difference in the ethnicity effects on Singaporean's first marriage timing (Sect. 3.3.4). As we noted in the Sect. 3.3.3, on the one hand, male Non-Chinese residents marry earlier than Chinese, however, this accelerating Non-Chinese effect loses statistical significance once controlling the immigration effects but not by schooling years nor special first occupations. On the other hand, there remains the promoting Non-Chinese effect for female Singaporeans after adjusting their birth country effects, while the birth countries outside of Singapore rise not only male hazard rates but also female first marriage rates similarly. We found these results after average marriage timings by gender (in baseline hazard functions of age as its argument) are adjusted with other covariates held fixed. In this sense, the ethnicity effects are gender specifics and the statistically significant gender difference in the ethnicity effect is genuine that is caused by noting other than ethnicity among covariates in the models. The genuine ethnicity effect may suggest a possible explanation by increasing phenomenon of inter-ethnic marriage. According to *Statistics on Marriages and Divorces*, Chinese males have more committed to inter-ethnic marriages than females did especially after the late-2000s: the proportions of Chinese husband who marry with Non-Chinese wife for 1965–1970, 1990–2000, and 2010–2015 are 0.7%, 3.8%, and 12.0%; the same proportions for female are 2.6%, 3.3%, and 6.8%, respectively. The surge of Chinese husband's inter-ethnic marriages must bring Non-Chinese wife's marriage and raises female's marriage rate. In the same period, international marriage increased substantially between a non-resident wife and a resident husband, which uplifted female's marriage rates. However, our estimation sample is consisted only of Singapore residents in addition to that the birth country effects were adjusted in the models, so possible explanations must resort to examining other factors than relying on international marriage that likely associates with immigration. In addition to the small size of usable cases, it limits further investigations that spouse's ethnicity was not collected in 2016OSMFW. We call a rigorous sensitivity analysis by using another large-scale survey on these issues. Nonetheless, inter-ethnic and international marriage may have become playing a significant role to determine future directions of Singapore marriage, fertility, and population structure.

In Singapore, extensions of schooling prevail among females more rapidly than among males, and female's proportions of higher education exceeded male's proportions in the youngest cohorts (Sect. 3.1.3). In the event history analysis, we found a gender equality in the education effects decelerating first marriage among male and female Singaporean (Sect. 3.3.4). By a composition effect, more female population attains higher education, female (gross) marriage rates suffer more than male's rates. It would be a rational reaction of Singaporeans to lowering female resident's nuptiality that foreign wives increased more rapidly than foreign husbands. In addition, the increasing international marriage may reflect prevalent traditional gender role of females. We found an insignificant gender difference in education effect such that higher education gave opportunity for a high-income job and decelerated marriages both males and females. At the same time, we found significant gender difference in special first occupation effect by which male specialist's marriage was accelerated later in their life course. Male Singaporean may search an opportunity outside Singapore for comparative advantage in household production that induces female specializing in non-market goods production but male specializing in labor supply. This specialization is more likely beneficial for couples with large wage differentials such as unskilled foreign wife and skilled husband. In the traditional world, only highly educated female may feel to owe opportunity costs if not sharing dividends of the household productions. Presumably, having a child, which is permitted within a formal marriage by Singaporean society, accounts a significant portion of net revenue in household production. Meanwhile the immigration policy effectively functions as a population stabilizing policy by stimulating international marriage, it was not admitted to remain long, given limited land space and difficulties harmonizing immigrants. When promoting early marriages, policy responses need to examine how efficiently and effectively eliminate opportunity costs of childrearing that are perceived by female citizens and permanent residents who pursue both productive economic activities and the traditional gender role.

Acknowledgements The author thanks Christopher Gee Kok Aun, Mui Teng Yap, Noriko Tsuya, Shigesaburo Kabe for helpful comments and suggestions.

References

Cox, D. R. (1972). Regression models and life-tables. *Journal of the Royal Statistical Society Series B (Methodological), 34*(2), 187–220.

Das Gupta, P. (1993). *Standardization and decomposition of rates: A user's manual* (pp. 23–186). U.S. Bureau of the Census, Current Population Reports, Series. Washington, D.C.: U.S. Government Printing Office.

Hajnal, J. (1953). Age at marriage and proportions marrying. *Population Studies, 7*(2), 111–136.

Saw, S.-H. (2007). *The population of Singapore* (2nd ed.). Singapore: Institute of Southeast Asia Studies Publishing.

Sun, S. H.-L. (2012). *Population policy and reproduction in Singapore: Making future citizens*. New York: Routledge.

Chapter 4
Where Have All the Babies Gone?—An Educational Perspective on Singapore's Low Fertility

SIM Choon Kiat

Abstract Issues related to fertility are matters of survival in small and resource-scarce Singapore. This is the reason why the city-state has a multi-track education system to enhance the quality of its people regardless of ability, race, gender or other factors. And to secure the quantity of its people, the island city also has various measures to support marriage, childbirth and child-rearing, and to take in immigrants and foreign workers. No doubt these policies have formed the foundation and push for Singapore's national building and development, they have however formed an unwavering "tournament competition mindset" among the people. Such a mindset is fostered through the competitive school system and extends even beyond adulthood. While it contributes to economic growth and prosperity, it inevitably causes endless stress and may well be the main reason behind low fertility in Singapore. The important question is thus how to strike the difficult balance between encouraging competition to promote excellence and checking low fertility. This is a dilemma that is difficult to solve yet inescapable and challenging. Societal mindset may take a long time to evolve, but it is high time for Singapore to plant something else in the hearts of its people to replace the "tournament competition mindset."

Keywords Education · Career · Meritocracy · Immigrants · Foreign workers · Demographic composition · Race · Stress · Fertility · Child-rearing · Tournament competition mindset

4.1 Three Tragic Characters in a Satire Stage Play

Back in my school days in Singapore, I was always one of the leaders of the theater group, acting on stage, directing or playwriting. I continued this childhood passion at a theater company even after I had become a civil servant with a statutory board

SIM C. K. (✉)
Showa Women's University, Tokyo, Japan
e-mail: simsimshowa@swu.ac.jp

S. Matsuda (ed.), *Low Fertility in Japan, South Korea, and Singapore*,
Population Studies of Japan, https://doi.org/10.1007/978-981-15-2830-9_4

under Singapore's Ministry of Education. I only ended this pastime interest in my early thirties when I changed my life direction and decided to pursue a Ph.D. in Sociology of Education. I wrote and acted in my last stage play named "Blowing in the Wind" in 2002, the year when I was already a master course student studying in Japan.

Apologies for the long introduction that intended to give the background of the three tragic characters which I satirically created in the play "Blowing in the Wind." The hapless trio, Mr. A, Ms. B and Mrs. C were all outcasts under the rule of a fictional totalitarian state (Country S) and had been pursued by the police for breaking laws.

Mr. A just could not pass the secondary school examination after numerous attempts. And, disastrously, he had reached the age of twenty-five, the eligible age limit for the fateful examination. Ms. B, though highly educated, was still single in her late thirties. And this was despite the government having tried countless times to matchmake her with potential partners. Mrs. C, although married for years, remained childless without legitimate reasons. And what was worse, she had already passed her reproductive years.

In trying to escape from the police, or perhaps under the influence of some magic blowing in a sudden gust of wind, the trio were desperately compelled to take a big turn in their lives. Mr. A finally decided to leave his beloved old mother and flee. Ms. B jumped into a tiger pit at the zoo where she was confronted by her ex-schoolmate who was then also a policeman. And Mrs. C tried to smuggle herself and her husband out of Country S at midnight, just like boat people.

Evidently, the above scenario is a satire of the social climate that prevailed in Singapore at the turn of the twenty-first century. While the epilogue of each character will be left to the imagination of the readers, my intention of highlighting this story is to show how low academic achievers, or highly educated single people, or childless married couples were regarded as "social untouchables" even in the year 2002. I made the following comments in an article about the play:

> In Singapore, the so-called underdogs are not just those with low education level. An unmarried single person is also seen as someone who is not contributing to the country. And even if you are married but not having children, it is as though you have been lazy and again not serving the country.
>
> —Translated from author's own comments made at *LianHe ZaoBao*, a local Chinese newspaper, published on August 18, 2002.[1]

[1]A newspaper article, in Chinese, that carried the story of the play and my comments as a playwright-cum-director-cum-actor can be found in the following Web site: http://call999.net/cgi-bin/czreadall.pl?mesgdir=messages&board=%B4%B4%D2%E2%C2%DB%CC%B3&User=&Pass=&file=193&records=18417&year=2002&month=08 (accessed March 15, 2019).

What made me utter these words about two decades ago? And why the issues concerning education, marriage and childbirth had and still hold such social magnitude in Singapore? The ensuing sections will answer these questions, using the examples of poor Mr. A, Ms. B and Mrs. C.

4.2 Mr. A: Convicted for not Meeting Educational Requirement

It is a well-known fact that the size of city-state Singapore is small. There is no arable land or natural resources to boot. Hence, to build its national wealth or even just to survive as a nation, it is imperative for and the destiny of Singapore to fully tap her only resource, which is its people (Sim 2009). Inevitably, Singapore must purposefully stretch the ability of its most-talented people while fully developing the potential of the rest, by providing the best possible educational opportunity to everyone.

It is against such a backdrop that Meritocracy (Young 1958) has always been the cornerstone of nation building, spearheaded by Mr. Lee Kuan Yew, the first and late Prime Minister of the Lion City, with his People's Action Party, which remains the only ruling party the country has ever known since its independence in 1965. Meritocracy, simply put, is a system that intends to sort and allocate social positions and roles according to one's IQ and effort, regardless of social background or parental influence. Meritocracy aims to maximize the overall quality of Singapore's people and at the same time ensure that the island state will be led by the cream of society.

Because of this, the education system of Singapore has adopted a multi-track approach since 1979. Under the so-called streaming system, as the name implies, children are canalized based on their school performance from as young as the fifth grade. As schools are either national/public or heavily funded by the government, all school goers are compelled to abide to this meritocratic system. Exceptions are only possible for students who have valid reasons to enroll in international schools, for example if they have spent their childhood overseas, or if their parents decide to emigrate and leave Singapore.

To ever upgrade the quality of its manpower, Singapore annually allocates the second-largest percentage (more than 20%) of total government expenditure in education, a proportion just below the amount spent on defense. Such is the extent and intensity that Singapore views the enhancement of human resources as one of the top national policies. Naturally, this national priority is shared by the citizens since almost all Singaporeans attend local schools and are thus socialized into accepting education as the paramount factor in ensuring continued national survival and prosperity. So, has Singapore reaped the fruits of its investment and succeeded in its ambition to achieving education excellence?

Table 4.1 Top five performers in TIMSS 2015 and PISA 2015

TIMSS 2015				PISA 2015		
Fourth grade		Eighth grade		Math	Science	Reading
Math	Science	Math	Science			
Singapore	Singapore	Singapore	Singapore	Singapore	Singapore	Singapore
Hong Kong	Korea	Korea	Japan	Hong Kong	Japan	Hong Kong
Korea	Japan	Taiwan	Taiwan	Macau	Estonia	Canada
Taiwan	Russia	Hong Kong	Korea	Taiwan	Taiwan	Finland
Japan	Hong Kong	Japan	Slovenia	Japan	Finland	Ireland

4.2.1 Singapore's Performance in Global Education Rankings

Both the Trends in International Mathematics and Science Study (TIMSS) and the Program for International Student Assessment (PISA) are the two international comparative studies in educational achievement that have gained much attention and interest globally in recent years.[2] The quadrennial TIMSS assesses fourth and eighth graders in math and science; whereas, the triennial PISA evaluates fifteen-year-old students' performance in math, science and reading. Coincidentally, 2015 saw the conduct of the two tests in the same year, and it turned out that Singapore became the first country in history ever to monopolize top spots in all seven categories, overshadowing traditionally high-performing economies such as Japan, Korea and Taiwan (Table 4.1).

The stellar performance of Singapore was widely published by almost all major newspapers around the world. As reported by BBC News on December 6, 2016, OECD education director Andreas Schleicher said Singapore was "not only doing well but getting further ahead."[3] Singapore was also highlighted as one of the academically top-performing "cleverlands" by Crehan (2017) in her well-acclaimed book of the same name.

The next section provides a brief overview of the IQ plus effort-based multi-track education system of Singapore to give a better picture on how the national policy of Singapore in maximizing the quality of its human resources influences one's life course.

[2]TIMSS is conducted by the International Association for the Evaluation of Educational (IEA), while PISA is administered by the Organization for Economic Co-operation and Development (OECD).

[3]More details of the report by BBC News can be read on the following Web site: https://www.bbc.com/news/education-38212070 (accessed March 15, 2019).

4.2.2 An Education System that Aims to Optimize Human Potential

Primary Education

As detailed by Crehan (2017) and Sim (2019), among others, all fourth graders at the compulsory primary level will take the school-based national examinations so that they can be grouped separately in each subject depending on how they perform academically, under a scheme known as "subject-based banding."

Also, though not mandatory, third graders at primary schools are "invited" to sit for a screening test that selects the top one percent of each cohort for the Gifted Education Program. As the name suggests, this program provides special education to gifted students and gives them the opportunity to stretch their abilities to the maximum. The majority of children take this test since most parents like to think that their children are gifted.

Under such circumstances, it does not take a genius to imagine how educational competition and the pressure that comes with it could affect young children and their parents even at the early stage of schooling.

Secondary Education

Streaming or grouping of students by IQ plus effort continues into the non-compulsory secondary level. However, students at this level are channeled into different courses instead of individual subject. Data in the "Education Statistics Digest 2017" (ESD 2017) published by the Ministry of Education indicated that usually about 98% of primary school students passed the Primary School Leaving Examination (PSLE), and the percentages of those who passed and enrolled in the Express and the Normal courses at secondary schools were around 60% and 40%, respectively, over the years.

Additionally, students who fail the PSLE twice can opt to progress to specialized secondary schools that provide technical training and prepare these students for entrance into the Institute of Technical Education years later. Therefore, almost all children in Singapore proceed to the secondary level of education, even though it is not a compulsory stage.

Further, while Express course students take the GCE "O" (Ordinary) level examination at the end of their four-year studies, those at the Normal courses will sit for the less demanding GCE "N" (Normal) level examinations. Students who perform well at the GCE "N" level will be given a chance to work hard for an extra year and take the GCE "O" level a year later.

There is thus essentially no cul-de-sac in the education system of Singapore. As Ng (2017) contends, the meritocratic education of Singapore is not an "unforgiving" one where the winners take it all and the losers take the fall. Rather, it is a "compassionate" meritocracy that leaves no child behind and allows the losers to still stand tall and hope for "restoration." This, on the other hand, means that competition continues through the endless provision of second, third chances or more. By analogy, such a system can be likened to a pressure cooker in which the pressure never drops.

In recent years, there is also a growing number of Specialized Independent Schools that impart a four- or six-year special training to students with special talents in fields such as the arts, sports, math, science or technology. Similarly, more combined schools are available to offer the Integrated Programs (alias "through-train" programs) to cater to the special needs of academically stronger students from the seventh to the twelfth grade. These schools allow students to skip the GCE "O" level and directly take the GCE "A" (Advanced) level or the International Baccalaureate (IB) examination, thus securing more room to implement a seamless and more holistic education for the students.

Consequently, this obviously adds pressure on students who aspire to enter these privileged schools and on their parents who wish likewise. Competition hence does not diminish but rather intensifies as one moves up the education ladder.

Post-Secondary Education

In a multi-track system, the type of course into which a student has been placed will inevitably determine his or her future path and destination. Except for the Specialized Independent Schools and combined schools with the Integrated Programs, there are basically only three types of post-secondary institutions to which a secondary school leaver can choose to progress, namely the Junior Colleges, the Polytechnics and the Institute of Technical Education (ITE). "ESD 2017" indicates that the percentages of the cohort in these institutions were 28.4%, 46.9% and 24.8%, respectively, in 2016, implying that almost all students in Singapore proceed to post-secondary studies.

Junior Colleges only take in GCE "O" level holders and prepare them for the GCE "A" level examination, which is the most common qualification for admission to local universities. The Polytechnics mainly accept students from the Express course and equip them with the necessary skills and knowledge to start work as technologists upon graduation. Graduates from the Polytechnics are given the Diploma in the field where they have been trained. ITE primarily provides technical training to school leavers from Normal courses and prepare them to work as technicians with national certificates in future.

According to the "ESD 2017," only about 34.2% of the cohort managed to secure a place at one of the local universities in 2016. Local universities are not accessible to ITE students, who may progress only to the Polytechnics if they perform well in their studies. Hence, there is a "consolation race" even for ITE students if they maintain their efforts to perform well from ITE to Polytechnics and then to the universities. As a result, competition never ends, and the pressure to stay ahead is always there, regardless of the level or type of student.

4.2.3 An Unwavering Tournament Competition Mindset

As described above, it is obvious that tests and examinations play important roles in Singapore's education system that aims to optimize human potential and at the same time select the best to lead the country into a brighter future. Under such an environment, it is no surprise that Mr. A in the satirical play "Blowing in the Wind" was convicted of continuously failing the secondary level examination, be it "O" or "N" level, even at the statutory age limit of twenty-five.

Moreover, as pointed out earlier, schools in Singapore are either national/public or are heavily funded by the government. School fees are thus made affordable to all citizens. On top of that, there exist many financial assistance schemes to help needy students who still face pecuniary challenges (Sim 2017). Simply put, though exaggerated in "Blowing in the Wind," with considerable support from the government of Country S and the setting up of courses and institutions for students with the least academic potential, Mr. A who continued to fail to meet the minimum educational requirement even at an advanced age of twenty-five was doomed to be labeled as someone who did not put in enough effort or refused to participate in educational competition.

The competition pattern of Singapore's education can be likened to the tournament mobility model, as advocated by Rosenbaum (1976). In this model, one must persist in competing at all selection stages so as not to be "weeded out" en route. One thus faces enormous pressure to remain in the tournament. Further, under the Singapore system, if one loses, he has no choice but to admit defeat by resigning to a less demanding course or take part in the "consolation race" and persevere in the competition.

And that is not all. As the progression rate to local universities stays at around 30% and wage disparity is closely linked to one's education level, competition not only does not abate but can also become more acute even after one has left school. As Low (2014) rightfully pointed out, "as with the logic of arms race, everyone suffers when we compete for relative position or status." And despite constant efforts made by the Ministry of Education to ease competition by emphasizing many pathways to success through corporate brochures and leaflets,[4] the heat of competition surrounding education never seems to cool down, with all aiming to achieve the so-called 5Cs of Singapore: Cash, Car, Credit Card, Condominium and Country Club membership.

The next section will examine how such "tournament competition mindset" still remains deep rooted and may be a possible reason behind Singapore's low fertility.

---

[4]Examples of such publicity can be read at the following links: https://www.moe.gov.sg/docs/default-source/document/about/files/moe-corporate-brochure.pdf, https://www.moe.gov.sg/microsites/cos2017/files/Budget2017-Infographic.pdf (both accessed March 15, 2019).

4.3 Ms. B: Wanted for Not Tying the Knot

Unlike Mr. A, Ms. B was highly educated. She was in the wanted list not because of her education but because of her singlehood.

The phenomenon of a growing number of highly educated unmarried women in their mid-late thirties, despite much persuasion and intervention from the government, is not new in Singapore and dated back to the 1980s. About thirty-five years ago, back in 1983, the late Mr. Lee Kuan Yew ignited "The Great Marriage Debate" in his National Day Rally speech when he brought the national attention to the issue of graduate women delaying or even forsaking marriage and childbirth. This was the first time when education was associated with fertility.

In his speech, Mr. Lee used data from the 1980 census to show that while uneducated women gave birth to an average of three children, women with higher education only produced 1.65 children (Saw 1990). He then cautioned that low fertility among the highly educated would cause a "thinning of the gene pool," and thus a national economic disaster (Lyons-Lee 1998). Not long after, Mr. Lee advocated eugenics, contending that highly educated and hence intelligent mothers produced intelligent children. Astonishingly, he even claimed that it might be a good thing that the Japanese allowed for secondary wives (Cheng 2017), though such practice was no longer common in Japan then.

Such eugenicist views naturally created controversy and invited repulsion even from women who were highly educated. Notwithstanding the backlash, numerous pro-natalist measures were introduced in the following years to address the lopsided procreation pattern in which better-educated women were delaying marriage and motherhood. These measures included providing tax rebates, childcare subsidies to parents who had given birth to a third child and priority to them if they wished to upgrade to a larger government flat.

Additionally, the Graduate Mothers' Priority Scheme was implemented to allow the third child of a graduate mother for prioritized entry into a primary school of choice (Shaddick et al. 2017). In any case, the slogan flagged by the then government was "Have 3, or more if you can afford it."

This slogan was apparently discriminatory as the other side of the coin seemed to suggest that "Do not have 3, if you cannot afford it." Besides, there was an undertone implying that only educated parents could benefit from the new measures since income level and thus "affordability" was and still is directly tied to one's education under Singapore's meritocratic system. As a matter of course, winners of the tournament competition should be awarded accordingly and rightfully. Therefore, it appeared Singapore only required highly educated women like Ms. B to be "fruitful, multiply and replenish its land."

Ironically, prior to the "The Great Marriage Debate" in early 1980s, family planning campaigns were launched by the now defunct Family Planning and Population Board to encourage delayed marriage and discourage big families. It is unthinkable now that the campaigns would urge people to take their time to say "Yes" to marriage and to stop at two children. I still remember clearly that no posters that cried out "Two is enough" had a boy's picture in them. Other anti-natalist slogans would include "The more you have—The less they get" and "Smaller Families—Brighter Future."[5]

Still more, a Social Development Unit (SDU) to help the singles find their lifetime partners was founded in 1984 immediately after Mr. Lee's national rally speech. Membership of SDU was however restricted to only male and female university graduates, as if its mission was to produce smarter babies. Education was still notably linked to procreation.

A year later in 1985, the Social Development section (SDs) was established to cater to non-university graduates with at least secondary qualifications, and in 1990, another Social Promotion section (SPs) was finally set up to matchmake an even larger number of individuals with less than secondary qualifications. Both the SDs and SPs were merged to become the Social Development Service (SDS) in 1995 to provide consolidated services to non-university graduates.

The history of the establishment and merger of official matchmaking units simply testifies to the decisive role of education in the entire process.

Nonetheless, Singapore, like many other advanced economies, soon witnessed a continual drop in fertility among women regardless of educational level. The situation became so serious that it left no room for concern over whether one was well educated or not and resulted in the amalgamation of SDU and SDS to become the new Social Development Network (SDN) in 2008.

The SDN was tasked to strengthen programs and initiatives that help singles connect and widen their social circle irrespective of one's educational background. Accreditation of private marriage agencies and matchmaking companies also became one of the SDN's new policies. Interestingly, it took more than a quarter of a century for the government of Singapore to finally delink education from its official dating services.

After many twists and turns, the SDN today remains committed to its initial mission of organizing events for singles to meet and interact, funding ideas from various organizations to create more opportunities for individuals to socialize and helping to develop the dating industry under its accreditation framework. All in all, with the support of taxpayers, the SDN continues to contribute to the country's fight against low fertility by "promoting marriages and nurturing a culture where singles view marriage as one of their top life goals."[6]

Sadly though, a survey conducted by the National Youth Council in 2016 showed that not many young Singaporeans, perhaps including Ms. B the "law-breaker," see marriage as one of their ultimate life goals (Table 4.2). Many youths, aged 15–34 years old, consider "to acquire new skills and knowledge," "to have a successful career" and "to earn lots of money" as very important life goals in their

[5]Interesting images of these posters can be googled simply by typing in the phrase "Two is Enough".

[6]When our research group visited Singapore in 2015, one of the SDN's mission statements was "to promote marriages and nurture a culture where singles view marriage as one of their top life goals," but this has been deleted from its official Web site.

Table 4.2 Singaporean youths' top ten "very important" life goals by age group

	15–19 (%)	20–24 (%)	25–29 (%)	30–34 (%)	Overall (%)
To have a place of my own	71	71	69	68	70
To maintain strong family relationships	73	69	68	69	70
To acquire new skills and knowledge	67	64	61	57	62
To have a successful career	71	63	55	49	59
To earn lots of money	47	46	46	43	46
To help the less fortunate	53	42	38	33	41
To contribute to society	52	42	36	31	40
To get married	34	35	37	38	36
To have children	30	31	36	41	35
To have a good personal spiritual/religious life	35	30	29	33	31

Source Adapted from "The State of Youth in Singapore 2017," National Youth Council, Singapore

lives, illustrating the eagerness to learn new things for the enhancement of career and income. And, evidently, such "tournament competition mindset" that spurs one to stay ahead in the rat race does not weaken much even among youths in their thirties.

Meanwhile, while the percentages of youths who choose "to get married" and "to have children" as their very important life goals increase slightly with age, they remain low as compared to goals formed under the influence of the "tournament competition mindset." What is more telling is that the above trend has not changed much ever since the same survey was first conducted in 2002.[7]

Notwithstanding or because of the efforts put in by the SDN, the total number of marriages in Singapore has generally increased modestly in the twenty-first century with the growth in population (Table 4.3). Marriage rates of both males and females have also slightly increased over the past decade, but the rate for females has constantly fallen below that of male. This is the very reason why one of the three main characters in the play "Blowing in the Wind" was set as Ms. B instead of Mr. B. Furthermore, females like Ms. B who "are highly educated but still single in their late thirties" remain large in number in Singapore (Tables 4.4 and 4.5).

Above all, while the unmarried rates of females are generally lower than those of males regardless of age group, the percentages of single females in their forties either come close to those of males in the same age group or has even surpassed them in 2016 (Table 4.4).

Worse still, the unmarried rates of females largely rise with highest qualification attained (Table 4.5). This is a trend exactly opposite to that observed for the males.

[7]The National Youth Council of Singapore conducted the same survey also in 2002, 2005, 2010 and 2013 and the details can be read at the following Web site: https://www.nyc.gov.sg/en/initiatives/resources/national-youth-survey/ (accessed March 15, 2019).

Table 4.3 Trends in the number of total marriages and marriage rate

	1970	1980	1990	2000	2010	2015	2016
Total marriages	14,572	22,444	23,953	22,561	24,363	28,322	27,971
Marriage rate (Per 1000 unmarried residents aged 15–49)							
Male	51.3	54.9	52.2	47.4	39.3	44.2	44.4
Female	65.3	67.3	59.2	46.8	35.3	41.1	41.6

Source Adapted from "Population Trends 2017," Department of Statistics, Singapore

Table 4.4 Percentage of singles among residents by age group and sex

Age group	1990		2000		2010		2016	
	Male	Female	Male	Female	Male	Female	Male	Female
30–34	34.0	20.9	30.7	19.5	37.1	25.1	37.7	26.5
35–39	18.1	14.8	19.7	15.1	20.4	17.1	21.2	17.5
40–44	10.9	11.5	14.8	13.6	15.3	14.1	14.6	15.0
45–49	8.5	7.3	10.5	12.5	13.2	12.8	12.6	12.9

Source Adapted from "Population Trends 2017," Department of Statistics, Singapore

Table 4.5 Percentage of singles among residents by age group, highest qualification attained and sex

Highest qualification attained	1990		2000		2010		2016	
	Male	Female	Male	Female	Male	Female	Male	Female
30–39								
Below secondary	29.6	12.9	32.3	11.4	32.7	10.6	36.8	13.0
Secondary	24.6	21.9	22.6	15.2	30.5	15.1	31.5	16.8
Post-secondary (non-tertiary)	22.9	27.3	22.6	19.3	30.1	19.4	29.2	18.0
Diploma and professional qualification	20.9	29.3	21.6	23.4	29.1	23.7	29.1	21.3
University	22.1	28.9	21.2	25.0	25.8	24.6	27.6	24.7
40–49								
Below secondary	11.8	7.1	17.4	8.5	20.4	9.0	19.9	8.8
Secondary	7.5	16.7	11.4	15.0	14.6	11.8	16.9	10.6
Post-secondary (non-tertiary)	8.5	19.1	9.3	16.9	14.2	14.4	15.7	10.3
Diploma and professional qualification	4.7	16.6	7.5	23.5	11.1	17.6	12.0	17.7
University	5.2	20.2	6.5	22.1	9.7	18.8	10.7	17.6

Source Adapted from "Population Trends 2017," Department of Statistics, Singapore

The percentages of single females in their forties with Diploma or higher qualifications, despite a slight improvement in recent years, continue to stay at a higher level. It is little wonder that the fictional government in Country S was so impatient with the case of Ms. B.

So why in the world are the singles, especially females like Ms. B, not married? And why should the government of Singapore spend national budget and so much effort in establishing a body like the SDN to promote marriage among them? The opinion survey conducted in Singapore by our research group may offer some hints to answering these questions. (Details of the research can be found in Chap. 3 of this book.)

When asked the question "why are you not married?," almost all of the 349 single people surveyed in our Singapore research, except for females in their forties, cited "because I want to devote myself to work or education now" as one of the three main reasons, regardless of age group, highest qualification attained or sex (Table 4.6). This undeniably suggests that the "tournament competition mindset" lives on even after one has left the school system. The pressure for better performance and higher achievement does not taper off but rather builds up as one ages.

As mentioned earlier, only 34.2% of the cohort managed to enroll in local universities in 2016. In contrast, data from the "Population Trends 2017" published by Singapore's Department of Statistics indicated that the proportion of university graduates among residents aged 25–34 and those aged 35–49 years old were 54.3% and 46.9% in 2016, respectively. This means that many people should have obtained their university degrees through foreign universities or at an older age after starting work. This again backs up the notion that the "tournament competition mindset" persists among young people even after entering the job market, just to enhance their credentials and thus market value.

Table 4.6 Top three reasons for being single by age group, highest qualification attained and sex

Age group/highest qualification attained	Male			Female		
	First	Second	Third	First	Second	Third
20–29	Work/ education	No money	No right person	Work/ education	No right person	Freedom
30–39	No money	Work/ education	No housing	No money	Work/ education	No right person
40–49	Work/ education	No necessity	No right person	No right person	Freedom	No social skills
Post-secondary (non-tertiary) or below	Work/ education	No money	No right person	No right person	No necessity	Work/ education
Diploma and professional qualification	No money	No right person	Work/ education	No money	Work/ education	No right person
University	Work/ education	No right person	No money	Work/ education	Freedom	No right person

Table 4.7 Percentage of respondents who agree to statements regarding marriage and childbirth by age group, highest qualification attained and sex

Age group/ highest qualification attained	Male			Female		
	Necessary or better to get married	Ought to have a child after marriage	Okay for unmarried couples to have children	Necessary or better to get married	Ought to have a child after marriage	Okay for unmarried couples to have children
20–29	66.9	89.6	74.3	61.8	86.2	73.1
30–39	79.0	90.3	72.9	70.4	90.3	60.6
40–49	75.7	90.9	64.5	70.0	93.0	46.7
Post-secondary (non-tertiary) or below	73.4	89.8	75.7	72.5	90.8	58.1
Diploma and professional qualification	75.1	91.2	69.1	68.0	87.8	60.7
University	72.4	89.6	67.3	63.4	90.7	60.0

Further, being married is a precondition for having children in Singapore (Table 4.7). That is also why the Singapore government is so adamant in getting the singles to first pair up and marry.

As noted earlier, very few young Singaporean view getting married or having kids as one of their important life goals. In connection with this, only 61–79% of all respondents to our research think that "it is necessary or better to get married," (Table 4.7) and it is naturally so since different people hold different values and priorities in life these days. However, about 90% of respondents in all age groups or education levels agree that one "ought to have a child after marriage."

On the contrary, not many respondents consider it "okay for unmarried couples to have children," especially among the females and those in their thirties and forties. Simply said, out-of-wedlock births are still not widely embraced. Therefore, it remains more socially acceptable for one Singaporean to get married first before he or she can be "fruitful, multiply and replenish" the land of Singapore. In other words, getting the singles to tie the knot is more of a pressing issue if the concern of low fertility is to be addressed.

From what have been discussed so far, it is reasonable to argue that the education differentials and "tournament competition mindset" that resulted from the multi-track system are important underlying factors which affect both marriage and childbirth rates in Singapore. By the same token, it is no wonder both Mr. A and Ms. B became outcasts in the fictional totalitarian Country S. They were convicted because they had betrayed the expectations of the country. One had continually failed in education and the other persistently refused to wed and procreate, despite an abundance of measures available to provide the necessary resources, opportunities and even rescue packages for the "academically challenged" students and "romantically challenged" singles.

The situation of Mrs. C was not any better. She and her husband had cleared both the educational and marital hurdles, and yet remain childless without valid reasons. Under the totalitarian rules of Country S, it is not difficult to imagine that they would be prosecuted and even persecuted socially, culturally and politically.

4.4 Mrs. C and Her Husband: Chased for not Reproducing

In resource-scarce Singapore, low fertility threatens to shake the keystone of national building. Hence, the pressure to "be fruitful and multiply" seems to have become one's obligation to the country. On the other hand, the government has also implemented a wide range of pro-fertility measures which include attractive baby bonus packages to lighten the costs of raising children and a slew of supportive pro-family leave schemes to offer more assistance for working parents (Sun 2012).[8]

In fact, as reported by the Straits Times on May 7, 2015, international aid agency "Save the Children" ranked Singapore fourteenth in the world and the best country in Asia to be a mother. The next best Asian countries were South Korea and Japan in the 30th and 32nd spots, respectively.[9]

And as anticipated and encouraged by the government, married females without children indeed belong to the minority (Table 4.8). Nevertheless, their proportion has been increasing over the years. In short, females like Mrs. C of Country S are on the rise in Singapore.

With the diversification of individual choices and life courses, and unless ruled under a totalitarian regime like Country S, certainly no judgement should be passed to childless couples like Mrs. C and her husband and have them labeled as being "reproductively challenged." Couples who choose not to have children must have their reasons to do so. Even so, securing the quantity of human resources is an equally if not more important issue in resource-deficient city-states such as Singapore.

The section below will look at some possible factors that may have influenced the decision of married couple not to procreate, based on the results of our research and analysis.

Firstly, among the top three most important policies that support child-rearing, respondents to our research chose the encouragement of flexible working patterns such as flextime or part-time work as a very important policy supporting child-rearing, especially by the mothers (Table 4.9).

[8]The many pro-family policies and programs initiated by the Ministry of Social and Family Development are also explained in details at the following Web site: https://www.msf.gov.sg/policies/Strong-and-Stable-Families/Supporting-Families/Pages/default.aspx (accessed March 15, 2019).

[9]The article by the Straits Times can be read at the following Web site: https://www.straitstimes.com/singapore/singapore-ranked-best-country-in-asia-to-be-a-mum (accessed March 15, 2019).

Table 4.8 Percentage of ever-married females who are childless by age group

Age Group	2000	2005	2010	2015	2016
30–39	14.1	17.9	20.1	20.7	20.3
40–49	6.4	7.0	9.3	11.6	11.4

Source Adapted from "Population Trends 2017," "Population Trends 2016" and "Population in Brief 2011," Department of Statistics, Singapore

Table 4.9 Top three most important policies supporting child-rearing by age group, highest qualification attained and sex

Age group/ highest qualification attained	Father			Mother		
	First	Second	Third	First	Second	Third
20–29	Reduce education costs	Provide housing assistance	Encourage flextime work	Reduce education costs	Encourage flextime work	Encourage pro-family workplace
30–39	Reduce education costs	Offer tax incentives	Increase childcare allowances	Encourage flextime work	Reduce education costs	Offer tax incentives
40–49	Reduce education costs	Increase job security	Provide housing assistance	Encourage flextime work	Reduce education costs	Offer tax incentives
Post-secondary (non-tertiary) or below	Reduce education costs	Increase job security	Provide housing assistance	Reduce education costs	Encourage flextime work	Provide housing assistance
Diploma and professional qualification	Reduce education costs	Encourage flextime work	Increase job security	Encourage flextime work	Reduce education costs	Provide housing assistance
University	Reduce education costs	Encourage flextime work	Encourage pro-family workplace	Encourage flextime work	Reduce education costs	Encourage pro-family workplace

Secondly, and even more significantly, it also tells that policies that help to reduce educational costs are considered as the most or second most important by both fathers and mothers, regardless of age group or highest qualification attained.

To fully tap its limited human resources, educational costs in Singapore have indeed been kept low. On top of this, besides offering a myriad of scholarships to eligible students and bursaries to needy individuals, the Ministry of Education also declares at its Web site that it "provides financial assistance to needy Singapore Citizen students… so that all Singaporeans, regardless of their financial background, can benefit from the best opportunities in education."

Under the Ministry's financial assistance scheme, students from poor families or large families with low per capita income are given full waiver of school fees, subsidies for taking public transport or school bus and even free textbooks and school attire. Various assistance schemes are also available to further support

Singaporean students who need additional financial help in publicly funded post-secondary education institutions.[10]

Such policies have surely borne fruit and resulted in the high enrollment rates at the various post-secondary institutions, as discussed earlier. However, the low costs of education are only applicable up to the Polytechnic level, as the cost of studying at a university may not be affordable to everyone.

For example, the National University of Singapore (NUS) charges an annual minimum tuition fee of 8,200 Singapore dollars (one Singapore dollar is about 0.75 US dollar as at March 2019).[11] In addition, there are other fees such as the student services fee and health service fee.

While NUS has made a promise at its Web site that it "understands the challenge of financing undergraduate studies and is committed to ensuring that no deserving student is denied admissions because of financial difficulty," the term "deserving" can be rather ambiguous and, as stated thus far, winning the "tournament" to become a "deserving" student at NUS has never been an easy task.[12]

However difficult that task may be, most parents, again regardless of age group and educational level, still expect their kids to attend university and will also support their children beyond university until they become economically independent (Table 4.10).

These observations should not be surprising. With a culture that stimulates a "tournament competition mindset" among the population starting from primary schools, it is just natural for any parent to want to give the best start in life for their children and to wish that they excel in everything they do. This often is fueled by the fear to "lag behind."

The above tendency is further confirmed when all parents cite school or university fees and private tutoring as one of the three largest economic burdens in raising their children (Table 4.11).

Ironically though, the low costs of education up to the Polytechnic level mean that parents with higher qualifications, and thus more financial resources, will be more able to provide additional and better education opportunities for their children beyond the school curriculum. Our research has supported this trend as a higher percentage of better-educated parents do send their children to tuitions or extra classes outside school (Table 4.10). This is a concern as it may further widen the gap between the haves and the have-nots, hence paralyzing social mobility and leading to social reproduction.

As previously indicated, smaller families were promoted and encouraged through anti-natalist slogans such as "The more you have—The less they get" and

---

[10]The declaration by the Ministry of Education and details of the various financial assistance schemes can be confirmed at the following Web site: https://www.moe.gov.sg/education/financial-assistance (accessed March 15, 2019).

[11]The tuition fees per annum at the various faculties of NUS are listed at the following Web site: http://www.nus.edu.sg/registrar/info/ug/UGTuitionCurrent.pdf (accessed March 15, 2019).

[12]The Web site that spells out the financial aid offered by NUS is as follows: http://www.nus.edu.sg/oam/financial-aid (accessed March 15, 2019).

Table 4.10 Percentage of respondents who agree to statements regarding child-rearing by age group, highest qualification attained and sex

Age group/ highest qualification attained	Father			Mother		
	Expect children to attend university	Will support children beyond university	Children in tuitions/ classes outside school	Expect children to attend university	Will support children beyond university	Children in tuitions/ classes outside school
20–29	81.7	80.4	50.1	86.6	80.2	32.1
30–39	90.7	85.1	52.4	89.6	90.0	56.7
40–49	84.2	88.8	73.8	86.9	92.2	67.7
Post-secondary (non-tertiary) or below	79.3	85.8	59.1	86.3	94.5	56.0
Diploma and professional qualification	84.2	76.2	68.4	84.9	79.1	56.3
University	91.1	90.3	70.0	91.0	88.6	68.9

Table 4.11 Top three largest financial burdens in child-rearing by age group, highest qualification attained and sex

Age group/highest qualification attained	Father			Mother		
	First	Second	Third	First	Second	Third
20–29	Childcare	Medical care	School/ university fees	Medical care	School/ university fees	Private tutoring
30–39	Childcare	Medical care	School/ university fees	Medical care	Childcare	School/ university fees
40–49	School/ university fees	Medical care	Private tutoring	School/ university fees	Private tutoring	Medical care
Post-secondary (non-tertiary) or below	School/ university fees	Medical care	Childcare	Medical care	School/ university fees	Private tutoring
Diploma and professional qualification	Medical care	Childcare	School/ university fees	Medical care	School/ university fees	Childcare
University	Childcare	School/ university fees	Medical care	Childcare	Medical care	School/ university fees

"Smaller Families—Brighter Future." These messages may have permeated the minds of people, and it is understandable that married couples may hesitate to have more children beyond their financial means. Moreover, the influence of the "tournament competition mindset" only makes married couples more reluctant to have large families, especially if they are determined to provide the "extra" to their children on top of normal school classes.

Likewise, for couples who are motivated to move ahead in their career or achieve work-life balance without being burdened by having children, it is highly possible that they may even give up on the idea of becoming parents at all. After all, as contended by Straughan et al. (2009), "they will stand to lose much more financially if they retreat from career investment." This may be the very reason why the number of childless married couples, like Mrs. C of Country S, is on the rise in Singapore.

4.5 The Other Issue Regarding "Headcount"

It is well known that Singapore is not only one of the most multiracial cities in the world, but also a country that welcomes immigrants and foreign workers. Against such a background, when it comes to issues concerning human resources, not only do the quality and the quantity of manpower matter, but the type is just as important.

The acceptance of immigrants and foreign workers in Singapore has undergone a complete change over the past decades (Table 4.12). However, as detailed in "Population Trends 2017," the numbers of foreign workers and residents include the dependents (17%), foreign students (4%) and fixed term contract workers who are in principle not allowed to marry in Singapore (56%).[13] Unfortunately, while the intake of foreign workers may help alleviate labor shortage in Singapore, it at the same time intensifies competition and exacerbates the spirit of wanting to win the "tournament."

Furthermore, the trends in the number of total marriages, marriage rate and percentage of singles among residents have revealed clearly that the presence of foreigners has not contributed much to solving the problems of declining marriage and low fertility (Tables 4.3, 4.4 and 4.5).[14] This is testified by the slow decline in resident total fertility rate (TFR) over the past years (Fig. 4.1). There are also gaps between races in terms of TFR, with the rate significantly higher for the Malays than the other races.[15]

Interestingly, an opposite trend is observed showing the percentage of Malay primary school students, who have passed the Primary School Leaving

[13]The Ministry of Manpower clearly spells out the eligibility and restrictions regarding the different types of foreign workers at its following Web site: http://www.mom.gov.sg/passes-and-permits (accessed March 15, 2019).

[14]Figures in Tables 4.3, 4.4, 4.5 and 4.8 include permanent residents who reside in Singapore.

[15]According to "Population Trends 2017," the ethnic composition of resident population (including permanent residents) was Chinese at 74.3%, the Malays at 13.4%, Indians at 9.0% and others at 3.2% in 2017.

Table 4.12 Change in Singapore's demographic composition (unit: '000 people)

	1970	1980	1990	2000	2010	2016	2017
Singapore citizens	1874.8 (90.4%)	2194.3 (90.9%)	2623.7 (86.1%)	2985.9 (74.1%)	3230.7 (63.6%)	3408.9 (60.8%)	3439.2 (61.3%)
Permanent residents	138.8 (6.7%)	87.8 (3.6%)	112.1 (3.8%)	287.5 (7.1%)	541.0 (10.7%)	524.6 (9.4%)	526.6 (9.4%)
Foreign workers/ residents	60.9 (2.9%)	131.8 (5.5%)	311.3 (10.2%)	754.5 (18.7%)	1305.0 (25.7%)	1673.7 (29.8%)	1646.5 (29.3%)
Total population	2074.5	2413.9	3047.1	4027.9	5076.7	5607.3	5612.3

Source Adapted from Population Trends 2017, Department of Statistics, Singapore

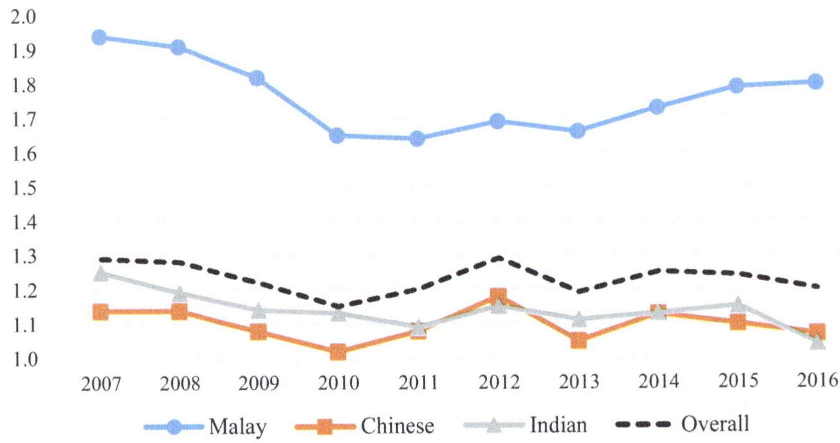

Fig. 4.1 Change in resident total fertility rate (TFR) by race. *Source* Adapted and created by author, as derived from Population in Brief 2013–2017, Department of Statistics, Singapore

Examination (PSLE) and are eligible for progression to Secondary School, lower than the other races (Fig. 4.2). While the low achievement in education among the Malays has been a long-standing social issue in Singapore, bringing much discussion in the educational, economic and even the political realms, there is still no established view regarding the contributing factors (Lai 2004; Kamaludeen et al. 2010; Tan 2013; Sim 2017).

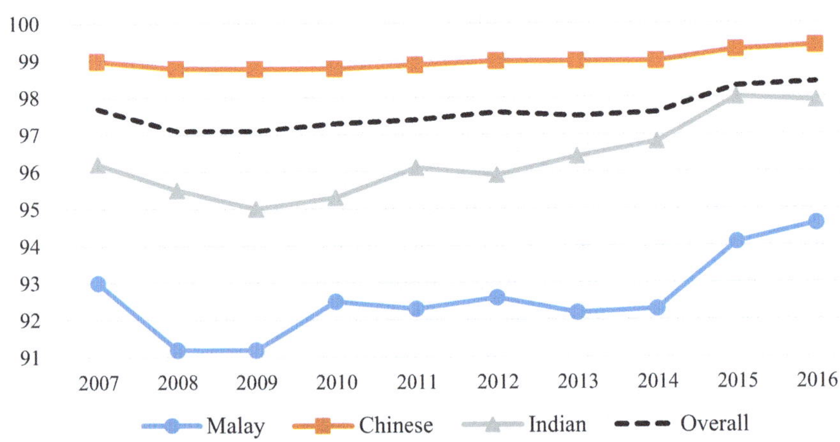

Fig. 4.2 Percentage of PSLE students eligible for secondary school by race. *Source* Adapted from Education Statistics Digest 2017, Ministry of Education, Singapore

There is certainly no evidence for correlation between the high TFR and the low educational achievement among the Malays, but the thought of "The more you have —The less they get" inevitably crosses one's mind. The message conveys a sense of reality especially under the effect of the "tournament competition mindset."

4.6 Concluding Thoughts

As deliberated thus far, issues related to manpower are matters of survival in resource-scarce Singapore. This is the reason why the city-state has introduced a multi-track education system to enhance the quality of its people regardless of ability, race, gender or other attributes. And to secure the quantity of its people, the island city has also implemented various measures to support marriage, childbirth and child-rearing, and to take in immigrants and foreign workers. These have formed the foundation and push for Singapore's national building and development.

However, the driving force behind the above measures is so strong that it has formed a steadfast "tournament competition mindset" among the people. This leads one to a possible conclusion that such underlying mindset may be the possible reason behind low fertility in Singapore, as discussed so far. The "tournament competition mindset," which is fostered through the school system and continues into working life, can be a double-edged sword. While it contributes to economic growth and prosperity, it no doubt also causes endless stress. And naturally, without a stress-free, or at least a stress-reduced environment, it will surely be difficult for the storks to bring babies to Singapore, even if monetary incentives and non-monetary support are sufficiently provided.

Where have all the babies gone? How to bring them back? Can Singapore wean itself off the reliance on competition for continuous economic success? There are no easy answers to these questions. The "tournament competition mindset" underpins and pervades the life of Singaporeans. To compete or not to compete: that is not the question, at least not in Singapore. The tiny country must survive.

The question then should be how Singapore can strike the difficult balance between encouraging competition to promote excellence and checking its low fertility. This is a dilemma that is difficult to solve yet inescapable and challenging. And unless a revolution happens, societal mindset will take a long time to evolve. Nonetheless, the writing is on the wall, and it is high time for Singapore to plant something else in the hearts of its people to replace the "tournament competition mindset," before it has to take drastic measures like the fictitious Country S.

Mr. Lee Kuan Yew who stirred up "The Great Marriage Debate" in the 1980s identified "population" as the issue that threatens Singapore's survival the most, in his book published just two years before his demise (Lee 2013). Lee, in the same book, argued that "What we really need in order to change the game is therefore a willingness to consider a different lifestyle and to have more babies."

Perhaps, Singapore should start to recognize that competition is not the only way to identify the survival of the fittest. An initial bold move to ease competition at schools may pave the path for the growth in fertility. Ultimately, it very much depends on how Singapore wants to shape its destiny as a country, rather than just grow the economy and win the future.

References

Cheng, U. W. L. (2017). AWARE—The early years. In C. Singam & M. Thomas (Eds.), *The Art of Advocacy in Singapore* (pp. 299–305). Singapore: Pagesetters Services.

Crehan, L. (2017). *Cleverlands: The secrets behind the success of the world's education superpowers*. Kansas City: Unbound.

Kamaludeen, M. N., Alexius, A. P., & Bryan, S. T. (2010). *Muslims in Singapore: Piety, politics and policies*. London; New York: Routledge.

Lai, A. E. (Ed.). (2004). *Beyond rituals and riots: Ethnic pluralism and social cohesion in Singapore*. Singapore: Eastern University Press.

Lee, K. Y. (2013). *One man's view of the world*. Singapore: Straits Times Press.

Low, D. (2014). Good meritocracy, bad meritocracy. In D. Low & S. T. Vadaketh (Eds.), *Hard choices: Challenging the Singapore consensus* (pp. 48–58). Singapore: NUS Press.

Lyons-Lee, L. T. (1998). The 'graduate woman' phenomenon: Changing constructions of the family in Singapore. *Sojourn: Journal of Social Issues in Southeast Asia, 13*(2), 309–327.

Ng, P. T. (2017). *Learning from Singapore: The power of paradoxes*. New York: Routledge.

Rosenbaum, J. (1976). *Making inequality: The hidden curriculum of high school tracking*. New York: Wiley.

Saw, S. H. (1990). *Changes in the fertility policy of Singapore*. Singapore: The Institute of Policy Studies.

Shaddick, E., Goh, L. S., & Oh, I. (2017). Against a teleological reading of the advancement of women's rights in Singapore. In Jiyoung Song (Ed.), *A history of human rights society in Singapore: 1965–2015* (pp. 132–149). London: Routledge.

Sim, C. K. (2009). *A comparative sociological study on the education system & meritocracy of Singapore: The socio-educational function & role of less selective schools (in Japanese)*. Tokyo: Toyokan Publishing.

Sim, C. K. (2017). Strategies for closing the achievement gap in Singapore: Approaches and challenges to ethnic differences (in Japanese). *Comparative Education: Bulletin of the Japan Comparative Education Society, 54*, 161–173.

Sim, C. K. (2019). How does educational selection in Singapore define what and how to test "merit"? In F. Onaka (Ed.), *Comparative sociology of examinations* (pp. 294–314). New York: Routledge.

Straughan, P. T., Chan, A., & Jones, G. (2009). From population control to fertility promotion: A case study of family policies and fertility trends in Singapore. In G. Jones, P. T. Straughan, & A. Chan (Eds.), *Ultra-low fertility in Pacific Asia: Trends, causes and policy issues* (pp. 181–203). New York: Routledge.

Sun, S. H.-L. (2012). *Population policy and reproduction in Singapore: Making future citizens*. New York: Routledge.

Tan, J. (2013). Singapore: The Malay Ethnic Minority—Playing perennial catch-up in education? In L. P. Symaco (Eds.), *Education in South-East Asia* (pp. 255–274). London: Bloomsbury.

Young, M. (1958). *The rise of meritocracy*. London: Thames & Hudson.

Epilogue

This book is the product of six years of collaborative research to clarify the status of and background for the low fertility rates observed in advanced Asian economies, such as Japan, South Korea, and Singapore, and the status of the countermeasures implemented by each country. As discussed in the preceding chapters, all the countries have expanded their countermeasures over a substantial period of time; however, this has not led to a significant recovery of the birth rate. Compared to when this study began, the total fertility rate in Japan and Singapore has hardly changed, and the birth rate has significantly decreased in South Korea. In such a situation, this book analyzes the reasons why each country's birth rate has not yet recovered, taking into account the social situation of and characteristics of the implemented countermeasures for each country.

The main findings of this research are as follows. Chapter 1 described the characteristics and problems of the countermeasures implemented in Japan against its low fertility rate. These measures were implemented from the 1990s through the first half of the 2010s. The Japanese government officially recognized the declining birth rate as a social problem following the "1.57 shock" in 1990, and since then, it has been implementing various countermeasures. The two pillars of these countermeasures against low fertility are increasing the number of childcare facilities and supporting a desirable work–life balance. The background of Japan's policies pertains to women's advancement in society; waiting for access to childcare facilities and encountering the difficulties in balancing work and childcare became social problems. Although countermeasures have steadily been progressing over the years, Japan's birth rate has not yet recovered. The reason is the mismatch between the main policy target of these countermeasures and the actual situations of families. The childcare facility and work–life balance policies mainly targeted dual-income couples working as regular employees; however, the needs of such couples are only part of the issue and the policies do not cover the needs of full-time homemakers and wives working as non-regular employees for short hours after childbirth. In addition, the rapid decrease in the marriage rate has significantly reduced the birth

S. Matsuda (ed.), *Low Fertility in Japan, South Korea, and Singapore*,
Population Studies of Japan, https://doi.org/10.1007/978-981-15-2830-9

rate; however, countermeasures against this decrease have been delayed. In other words, the birth rate did not recover because the countermeasures targeted only specific groups.

Chapter 2 investigated the determinants of the gap between attitudes toward the desired number of children and actual/expected number of children in Japan and South Korea. South Korea experienced a significant change in birth rate over a shorter period compared to Japan, and to adjust to this change, the South Korean government changed its population policy from being anti-natalist to pro-natalist. Since the mid-2000s, it has undertaken various countermeasures for low fertility rates, including removing the obstacles to birth and child-rearing, normalizing the work–family balance, and fostering a happy society for children. One of the most important countermeasures implemented by Japan and South Korea is the facilitation of work–life balance for the parents, particularly mothers, of young children, since, in both countries, women have difficulty balancing work and child-rearing efforts. Further, to enable women to achieve work–life balance, South Korea improved many of its systems, such as maternity leave, childcare leave, paternity leave, shorter working hours, and nursing leave to care for sick children. However, as explained in Chap. 2, these employee benefits unfortunately had no effect on the gap between desired and actual/expected number of children; that is, the work–life balancing measures did not make it possible for people to have their ideal number of children. In this issue, Japan's results overlap with the results presented in Chap. 1. Regarding South Korea, further analyses suggest that the intense competition for educational achievement, accompanying burden of educational expenses at home, and ever-worsening environment for young people are significant reasons for the low birth rate. Therefore, improving educational competition, reducing the burden of educational expenses, and improving employment opportunities for youth should have a greater impact on the birth rate than the current strategy of providing support to people to balance work and childcare efforts.

Using both macro- and microdata, Chap. 3 analyzed the changes in birth rate and their determinants in Singapore. The results revealed that nuptiality, rather than marital fertility, is the main driving force behind the changing birth rates for all the major ethnic groups in Singapore. The results also showed that the timing of the first marriage was significantly late for highly educated individuals and those pursuing managerial, professional, and special first occupations.

Chapter 4 examined the reasons for the decline in marriage and birth rates in Singapore from the perspective of the education system and subsequent career development. Unlike in Japan and South Korea, the deterioration of employment opportunities for young adults and the accumulation of the burden of educational expenses on parents are not the reasons for the declining marriage and birth rates in Singapore. This is because the Singapore government has made sufficient investment in education, and hence, the country's educational costs are low. Further, the national level of education is high and the employment environment for young people is stable. Therefore, why are the country's marriage and birth rates declining? To answer this question, this chapter explains that Singapore's young gain a "tournament competition mindset" through intense academic competition and subsequent career competition. Since this mindset emphasizes competition in terms of educational achievement and occupational status, but not marriage, young people choose to remain unmarried, causing a decline in the birth rate.

The aforementioned findings offer suggestions to improve the countermeasures against decreasing birth rates in not only the three Asian countries mentioned here but also other Asian countries/regions with low fertility rates. First, Japan's experience suggests that countermeasures against fertility rates do not affect the restoration of birth rate unless the policy's target matches the real situations of young and child-rearing households. Although implementing a policy to support childcare for regularly employed working couples will certainly benefit them, the same benefit does not extend to non-regularly employed couples, full-time homemakers, or single individuals. Moreover, targeting a wider population would definitely restore the overall birth rate. Hence, the best solution might be policies that implement countermeasures that, for example, allow each family to nurture and raise as many children as desired based on the variation of households in the parenting life stage.

Second, to recover their birth rates, Asian countries should mitigate the ongoing decline in marriage rates. This analysis of Singapore in this book showed that most of the decline in birth rates is caused by people choosing to remain unmarried. According to previous research, the situation is similar in Japan and South Korea. Accordingly, the most important countermeasure against low fertility rates is to make it easier for young people to get married.

Third, the so-called tournament competition mindset, which may have lowered Singapore's birth rate, may not be limited to Singapore alone. The educational competitiveness among children, which transforms into career competitiveness among young adults after graduation, is as intense in Japan and South Korea as it is in Singapore. Therefore, the tournament competition mindset might be a valid mechanism explaining the low birth rates in Japan and South Korea, as well as Singapore. However, research on the influence of this mindset is currently ongoing. The future challenge of such inquiries is expanding to include other Asian countries/regions with declining birth rates and examining in detail the situations and backgrounds of low birth rates to find appropriate countermeasures.

This book discussed the characteristics of and countermeasures against the low fertility rates of three Asian developed economies. We hope that the findings and implications of this research will provide new perspectives for researchers in this field.

Shigeki Matsuda

The manufacturer's authorised representative in the EU is Springer
Nature Customer Service Centre GmbH, Europaplatz 3, 69115 Heidelberg,
Germany. If you have any concerns regarding our products, please
contact ProductSafety@springernature.com

Printed and bound by CPI Group (UK) Ltd, Croydon, CR0 4YY
25/09/2026
02222891-0015